Cruises

How to choose . . .

Where to go . . .

What to do . . .

**Anne Vipond
& William Kelly**

Thomas
Cook

First published in the United Kingdom by
Thomas Cook Publishing
PO Box 227
Peterborough PE3 8BQ
United Kingdom

ISBN 0 906273 81 1

Managing Editor: Stephen York
Copy-editor: Annie Kay
Designed by Thomas Cook Design Studio
Typeset by Thomas Cook Publishing
Cover design by Thomas Cook Design Studio
Front cover photography by Tim Brightmore
Maps by Ocean Cruise Guides Ltd
Printed and bound in Great Britain by Bell & Bain Ltd, Glasgow

Contents

Acknowledgements

The authors and publishers wish to thank Joanne Field and Cris Rees of Thomas Cook Retail Marketing, and Sheena Noakes, the Manager of Thomas Cook, Richmond, Surrey, for their assistance and advice in the preparation of this book. The following individuals and organisations kindly supplied the photographs, and their co-operation is acknowledged with thanks.

Between pages 16 and 17: William Kelly; Anne Vipond; Royal Caribbean Cruise Line; William Kelly; Holland America Line; William Kelly; Princess Cruises.
Between pages 32 and 33: Cunard; Carnival Cruise Lines; Princess Cruises; Thomas Cook Holidays; Alaska Sightseeing/Cruisewest; TTB/Windstar Cruises.
Between pages 48 and 49: William Kelly; William Kelly; Anne Vipond; William Kelly; Anne Vipond; Royal Caribbean Cruise Line; Royal Caribbean Cruise Line; Crystal Cruises.
Between pages 80 and 81: Anne Vipond; AA Photo Library; AA Photo Library; AA Photo Library; Crystal Cruises; AA Photo Library; Thomas Cook Holidays.
Between pages 112 and 113: Royal Caribbean Cruise Line; Royal Caribbean Cruise Line; Crystal Cruises; Crystal Cruises; P & O Cruises; Royal Caribbean Cruise Line; Princess Cruises; Hong Kong Tourism Association.
Back cover: Daily Telegraph Picture Library.

About the authors

Anne Vipond and William Kelly are travel writers with a specialist interest in cruises. Based in Vancouver, they have visited some of the world's most exotic destinations in the course of their cruising voyages. A husband-and-wife team, they have collaborated on numerous articles on cruises for newspapers and magazines.

They are also the authors of two other books in the Thomas Cook Touring Handbooks series, *Cruising around Alaska* (published June 1995) and *Cruising around the Caribbean* (for publication in June 1996).

Introduction

Part of the reward of travel is the journey itself, and one of the best ways to see the world is by cruise ship. Cruising is a carefree mode of travel that leaves you relaxed and refreshed to enjoy each port of call; no other type of holiday enjoys a higher rate of customer satisfaction. In fact, the majority of first-time cruisers report that their inaugural voyage didn't simply fulfil their expectations, it exceeded them. The reason for this is the diversity of cruising. Talk to ten different people who took the same cruise and you will swear they took ten different holidays. Each passenger is free to do whatever he or she desires in the course of a cruise. Those who like to be active can take part in a jam-packed daily schedule of events, while those who prefer quieter pastimes can simply recline in a deck chair and gaze at the passing scenery.

More than 300,000 British holidaymakers took a cruise last year – many of them for the first time – yet others are still not tempted. They perceive cruising as being snobbish, expensive, sedate and boring. Many of these misconceptions are based on what cruising was like in the past, not the present reality. Over the past decade the cruise industry has transformed itself, and what was once an exclusive type of holiday has become an affordable and all-inclusive holiday package. Today's modern ships offer a wide range of itineraries and destinations, and an impressive array of optional activities, both on board and on shore.

Nonetheless, it's only natural to be sceptical about the unfamiliar. Those who have never cruised may think that cruise travel has nothing to offer except regimented activities. Then they embark on a first cruise and their conversion is instant – but by no means unique – as they stand at the rail waving farewell to those gathered at dockside. In the course of a cruise, this excited anticipation gives way to a serene self-indulgence as they sit down to yet another delicious meal, their appetites sharpened by the sea air.

The adventure and allure of cruising begins the moment a person walks across the gangway and steps onto a ship. Greeted by smiling faces and smartly attired stewards, each passenger feels special as he or she is welcomed aboard and shown to their cabins. The excitement of embarkation is surpassed only by the euphoria that fills the air when the lines are tossed and the ship eases away from the dock. There's an incomparable sense of freedom as the bonds of land are broken and those left waving from shore wish they were the lucky ones at the ship's rail, experiencing that magical moment when a ship sets sail for distant lands.

Cruising, as its growing popularity proves, provides both the adventure of travel and the relaxation of a pampered holiday. Passengers can visit the world's famous capitals and exotic ports of call, then retreat from the heat, hustle and bustle when they return to their ship – an oasis of calm and comfort wherever it may be docked.

This handbook has been designed to explain why cruising is one of the most satisfying modes of travel available to today's holidaymaker, and why cruise ships evoke a timeless appeal that is stronger than ever.

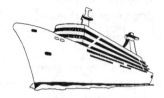

1 Why cruise?

The reasons for choosing to cruise are numerous, starting with the fact that cruising is one of the best value-for-money holiday packages available today. Other benefits are more abstract, such as cruise holidays providing a healthy release from modern-day stresses. And while individual passengers have their own personal reasons for cruising, the following are some of the benefits most often cited by cruise holiday-makers.

The ultimate in pampering and relaxation

We all need to occasionally 'get away from it all' and cruising literally removes you from all land-based routines and places you in a novel setting that is stimulating yet familiar, soothing yet engaging.

Cruising is hassle-free, crime-free and stress-free. Tired of making decisions? Envisage an evening at sea and its similarities to enjoying a night on the town at a popular holiday resort. Start with dinner at an elegant restaurant followed by a stage show, or dancing to a live band at a local club, or going to the cinema, or reclining in the corner seat of a piano bar, or browsing in the local shops, or trying your luck at a casino. These are all activities you can enjoy on board a cruise ship, but not once do you need to reach for your wallet, make a reservation, stand in a queue, pay a cover charge at the door, hail a cab, hand someone a tip, park your car or drive back to your hotel in the dark along unfamiliar streets. You can simply meander from venue to venue on board the ship, and if none of these activities suits your fancy on any particular evening, you can simply go for a late night stroll along the promenade deck, breathing in the fresh sea air before retiring to your cabin, which your steward will have tidied while you were at dinner, replacing used towels with fresh ones, turning down your bed, perhaps even placing a good-night chocolate on your pillow.

Sound idyllic? There's more. Daytime on board a ship is equally relaxing. Early risers can enjoy the dawn while striding the freshly scrubbed and sun-warmed decks. Breakfast can be enjoyed in bed, in the main dining room or outside on the lido deck. (See the Glossary on p. 140 for an explanation of this and other cruising technical terms.) You can sleep until noon if you like – your steward won't disturb you. On a cruise, your time is your own to do with as you please.

Do you fancy spending the morning in a deck chair by the swimming pool, dozing in the sunshine and going for a dip from time to time to cool off? Perhaps you would rather book an appointment at the beauty salon for a massage, facial and hair styling. Or maybe a vigorous workout is what you need to get all that work-related stress out of your system before sitting down to lunch. Whatever your definition of 'relaxation', it takes on its full meaning in the course of a cruise.

In our increasingly fast-paced world, cruising also provides the rare opportunity to slow down. No excuses are necessary to stretch out in a deck chair and indulge in daydreams as you gaze seaward at some billowy white clouds becalmed on a sea blue sky.

Family freedom

As much as we value the company of our loved ones, it's also nice to have some time to ourselves. On a cruise, couples and families can holiday together but still pursue their personal interests – both on board the ship and at each port of call.

For instance, one member of a couple may want to indulge in a nap after lunch while the other decides to take in a film at the ship's cinema. Or one of you may be interested in attending a lecture or an art auction, while your partner would prefer chipping golf balls or joining a table tennis tournament. It's easy to go your separate ways for a while, then rendezvous back at the cabin or in your favourite bar. Even at the ports of call, where the cruise lines offer organised shore excursions, one of you may choose to go on a city or island tour while the other would rather play a round of golf or spend an afternoon scuba diving. Of course there are many things you will want to do together, as a couple or a family, but on a cruise you also have the option of indulging your personal pleasures and interests. (For more information on the wide range of activities, see pp. 42–43.)

If you have brought children along, it could be hours before you see them again because they will be too busy having fun at the various shipboard facilities to pester their parents – or other passengers for that matter. Adults cruising without children have reported that although the ship was carrying a few hundred junior passengers, they hardly ever saw or heard them.

A cruise is one of the best types of holiday on which to take children. They are kept so busy and entertained, that it's not unusual for those who have been on a holiday that combined a trip to Florida's Walt Disney World with a Caribbean cruise to report that they enjoyed the cruise more!

Romance

Cruising is the perfect way to celebrate a marriage or wedding anniversary. Honeymooners are given the royal treatment on board a ship, often being invited to a private Captain's cocktail party or receiving a complimentary bottle of bubbly in their cabin. But apart from any special touches provided by the cruise line, the general ambiance of a cruise ship is ideal for a romantic interlude.

The connection of cruises with romance is familiar to us all from countless books and films. Strolling the decks together under a starlit sky, watching the sun set as you linger at the ship's rail, ordering breakfast in bed each morning, sharing an intimate table for two in the dining room each evening, lingering in a cosy corner of your favourite bar – there's no end to the romantic moments a couple can share on board a cruise ship.

Security and sense of community

There is, on board a ship, a wonderful feeling of community and security which is hard to duplicate on land. With most passengers boarding on the same day, wandering at ease throughout their floating resort and sharing their common experiences with fellow passengers, a true sense of community pervades the ship. People do not hesitate to smile, say hello and even share an impromptu joke with one another.

In most public settings, people remain somewhat wary of strangers. This is not the case on a cruise, however, because the ship remains off limits to the public at large. Passengers, crew and authorised shore personnel are the only ones allowed free access and, upon boarding a ship, people soon lower their guard and raise their standards of politeness in keeping with proper shipboard etiquette. The ship's captain and hotel manager set the standard of gracious behaviour, warmly greeting each and every passenger who chooses to attend the gala welcoming party. Their respectful demeanour is reflected in the hotel staff who pamper passengers with friendly and courteous service. The atmosphere this creates is not stilted or stuffy but one of genuine cheerfulness and common courtesy. It's hard for anyone to misbehave in such a pleasant environment.

Security on board a ship is unobtrusive. After initial embarkation, at which passengers and their luggage go through standard airport-style security checks, you simply present your identification card (issued to you at the start of the cruise) when re-embarking at each port of call. The ship's security officer is often positioned at the gangway, but he and his staff conduct most of their duties in a very low-key manner.

Perhaps one of the most appealing aspects of cruising, especially for women, is being able to wander throughout the ship's public areas at any time of day or night and not be worried about personal safety. With approximately one crew member for every two or three passengers, there are always staff on hand to lend assistance in any type of situation. And women on their own can feel totally at ease in the ship's bars, nightclubs and casino, secure in the knowledge that anyone they meet is a fellow passenger.

This feeling of security extends to parents travelling with children. They can let their children wander off to the playroom without worrying that they will become lost or frightened. And children welcome the novelty of being independent of their adults as each age group pursues its own organised activities.

Friendships that develop on a cruise are often fleeting but some do endure. New friends are easily made in this warm, friendly and relaxing atmosphere, whether it be a fellow 'regular' at your favourite bar or the engaging couple you share a dinner table with each evening. On the last night of a cruise it's not unusual to see fellow passengers hugging one another good-bye and exchanging addresses. Whether or not they ever see each other again, passengers will often say that the people they met on board were an important factor in their enjoyment of the cruise.

Passengers on a river vessel also enjoy a sociable atmosphere. Everyone on board shares a common interest in the history and culture of the area they have chosen to visit and this makes for easy conversation in the restaurant, bar and observation lounge.

Reliability

At first glance the cruise industry appears to be a complexity of ships and itineraries. Yet, in true naval tradition, the cruise industry is highly regulated and maintains stringent standards. Most ships are annually rated by various cruise experts, and travel agents have each ship's specifications at their fingertips. This allows your travel agent to recommend a particular cruise line or cruise ship with complete confidence that it will provide a pre-established level of accommodation, service, cuisine and other on-board amenities.

Thus there are rarely any unpleasant surprises for the consumer. In fact, not only can you learn exactly what facilities your ship of choice contains, the level of service to expect, the nationality of the officers and hotel staff, and the atmosphere (i.e., casual, semi-formal or formal) of the ship, you can also ascertain beforehand the exact size, layout and location of your cabin.

Meals are no mystery either. If you choose to sail on a British ship for instance, much of the food will be familiar fare regardless of the part of the world you are cruising. And for passengers with diverse culinary tastes, the tantalising selection of dishes will keep your palate stimulated. No one goes to bed hungry. In addition to breakfast, lunch and dinner, offerings often include afternoon tea, poolside barbecues and midnight buffets, not to mention room service.

Cruising is well known for the large quantity and high quality of food served on board; the standards of cleanliness on a cruise ship are also legendary. Your cabin steward will clean your stateroom twice a day and is always nearby to attend to any additional requests. The public areas are also kept spotless, with tables instantly cleared of used dishes, the decks constantly scrubbed and the brass always polished.

Last but not least, the ships' itineraries are established well in advance and described in detail, so that you know what ports of call are included in a particular cruise and can ascertain the estimated time of arrival and departure at each destination, and which days are spent at sea. This allows you to plan your holiday long before you board the ship.

Variety of shipboard facilities

Old meets new on today's cruise ships. The refined elegance of yesteryear is still evident in grand foyers and spacious dining rooms, but gone are the segregated public areas and three classes of passengers. Today everyone cruises first-class (although a few ships, such as the QE2, have different levels of dining room service, depending on the grade of cabin booked: for more details see Chapter 5).We can all enjoy the on-board amenities for which modern ships have been described as floating resorts.

Standard features now include at least one swimming pool, if not two or three, often with one located out of doors and another one either enclosed or covered by a Perspex roof that opens and closes depending on the weather conditions. A whirlpool and sometimes a paddling pool are usually located nearby.

The upper decks are also where passengers will find a jogging track, games court and possibly a golf putting green or net-enclosed driving range. A gymnasium is another popular facility, complete with exercise equipment, as is a health spa with sauna and steam room. Most ships also contain a beauty salon and hairdressers.

For passengers looking to improve their minds as well as their bodies, the ship's library will probably contain a good selection of reference material as well as bestselling paperbacks. A card/games room is often part of or adjacent to the library.

The shops on board usually include a few boutiques carrying designer jewellery, perfume and fashions, as well as a selection of drinks, all at duty-free prices. Basic toiletries can also be purchased on board, in case you forgot to pack your toothbrush or razor.

On-board services usually include a laundrette (with iron and ironing board) as well as a dry cleaners. At the photo shop you can purchase prints taken of you and your cruise companions by one of the ship's photographers. You can also have your own print film developed on board. The ship's doctor and nurse can be consulted at the medical centre, and a number of ships provide a playroom, night nursery and babysitting services.

Looking for entertainment? Then you've come to the right place. Most modern ships have a cinema, a casino, a show lounge where musicals and cabaret revues are staged each evening, and numerous bars with musical entertainment ranging from disco to classical.

Range of activities

Before we begin reviewing the dozens of activities – both group and individual – that are available to cruise passengers, let us first stress that you are free to participate as much or as little as you desire. There is absolutely no pressure placed on anyone to join in any activities taking place on board the ship, and it's quite easy for passengers seeking peace and quiet to find a corner in a lounge or an empty deck-chair from which to watch the scenery, read a good book or engage in conversation. The pace you choose to pursue on board a ship is entirely under your control.

That said, it should also be noted that the ocean liner days of pipe-smoking gents and long-skirted ladies playing a genteel game of shuffleboard have given way to casually clad passengers stretching and bouncing to the urgings of an aerobics instructor. Fitness programmes have become a standard feature on many modern ships and they include aerobics classes, hydro-calisthenics and work-outs on computerised exercise equipment.

Jogging usually takes place on the sports deck, leaving the promenade deck to those who prefer walking, strolling or simply leaning on the ship's rail with a drink in hand. Basketball, volleyball and table tennis tournaments are arranged by the cruise director's staff, as are clay pigeon shooting, deck football and cricket. And yes, shuffleboard is still played on most ships.

All this non-stop activity may sound a bit exhausting to some, but they need not worry. Less vigorous activities also abound, such as crafts sessions and fashion shows. And those looking to pamper themselves (and willing to pay for personal services) can indulge in a massage, facial and new hair-style in the ship's beauty salon. (For details on personal services and items not included in the price of a cruise, see Chapter 6, *Your cruise holiday*.)

On days when the ship is at sea there are a number of activities taking place simultaneously, including lectures on the next ports of call and the shore excursions being offered at each destination. These lectures are also replayed throughout the day on one of the channels featured on your cabin's television, if your cabin contains this amenity. Often films are also shown on cabin televisions as well as in the ship's cinema. Each day's movie schedule is posted in the daily programme that is slipped under your door.

The daily programme keeps you informed of all activities planned for each day, including religious services, and it soon becomes apparent that no passenger could participate in every event unless they stayed on board for a few months and tried new activities every day.

Of course, many passengers choose not to join in any of these organised activities. Individual pastimes can be pursued at your leisure, whether it's checking a book out of the library or lazing by the pool or enjoying a lemonade on the lido deck while the ship's band plays some sail-away tunes as the ship pulls away from a port of call.

The days, both at sea and in port, can be as busy or as restful as you like. And the same holds true for evening entertainment. You can take in the stage show every night, enjoying musicals that rival those of the West End and Broadway, and cabaret revues featuring talented comedians, singers, jugglers and magicians. Or, should you be in a mellow mood, you can enjoy after-dinner drinks to the melodious sounds of a string quartet or settle into a corner seat of a cosy piano bar. Those who like to be active can play the slot machines in the casino or go dancing in a nightclub or try singing in a karaoke bar. Passengers soon learn where the busy areas of a ship are at certain times of the day, where the quiet areas are, and everyone gravitates to the area and activity of preference that appeals to them.

Opportunity to pursue a special interest

A number of cruise lines now offer special cruises featuring guest hosts who are experts in a particular field. Their talks, clinics, performances and hosted tours ashore cover interests as diverse as bridge and birdwatching, golf and gardening. Photography buffs can learn helpful tips from the professionals and bridge players can book onto special cruises that feature a full EBU-licensed congress afloat.

Classical music voyages are popular theme cruises, their celebrity-hosted concerts featuring acclaimed musicians, as are jazz festivals at sea. Dance enthusiasts will be tempted to book onto cruises offering sequence dancing or Scottish highland dancing complete with dance champions and radio/TV recording bands. Even arts and crafts festivals, hosted by television personalities, are offered on special sailings.

River cruises are noted for their knowledgeable hosts – experts in their academic fields – who provide passengers with fascinating historical and cultural background on the lands they are cruising past and the ports of call. One of the best examples of this is a journey along the Nile, where excursions to view the great pyramids and temples of ancient Egypt are part of the cruise package.

Visiting many destinations in one holiday

People often choose a cruise based on the destinations included in the itinerary. Cruising offers them the opportunity to visit a variety of countries and capitals without ever changing hotels. Not only are they saved the hassle of packing and unpacking as they travel from one destination to another, they do not have to deal with foreign and fluctuating currencies except for incidental expenses incurred on shore such as shopping purchases or cab rides. Clearing each country's customs and immigration department is usually another hurdle handled by the ship's staff, with the entire passenger list quickly cleared with authorities as soon as the ship docks.

Many who travel by ship will say that nothing compares with a seaborne landfall. Whether it's watching the sun rise above a tropical island as your ship approaches its lush shores or seeing the sights of a bustling harbourfront draw ever closer as your ship glides into one of the world's famous ports, arriving by sea is a travel experience of unparalleled romance and timelessness.

The early risers will be out on deck to watch their ship pull into port. With courtesy flags raised, the ship sidles up to the dock where shore workers wait for the crew to toss them docking lines, their heavy rope eyes slipped onto huge cleats as a handful of curious passengers watch from the decks above. Once again the ship is linked to land, her passengers eager to disembark and explore the exotic destination to which their ship has brought them.

The world's great cities were built beside oceans and rivers, and their universal appeal – both as centres of commerce and as tourist meccas

bove Setting sail for foreign ports never fails
o excite even the most experienced cruise
olidaymaker. Here the Sun Viking departs for
he first Alaska cruise of the season.
ight The peace of an ocean sunset is a
aditional pleasure that is common to all
ruises.

Activities can be as energetic or relaxing as you wish. **Above** The fitness centre on the Royal Caribbean Cruise Lines ship Legend of the Seas. **Below** Ship's pool on the Windward. **Opposite** Scuba diving off Grand Cayman on a cruise with the Nieuw Amsterdam (Holland America Lines).

By taking a cruise you can sample a wide variety of exotic destinations, such as St Lucia in the Caribbean, and visit the world's great cities from the comfort of a luxurious 'floating hotel', like the Royal Princess (Princess Cruises) seen here in the lagoon of Venice.

– often translates into high prices for hotels and restaurant meals. Yet people travelling on cruise ships and river vessels needn't worry – their floating hotel will take them to some of the world's most expensive cities for a fraction of what it would cost if they were staying on shore.

Cruise ships and river boats take advantage of centuries-old transportation routes and their passengers travel at a relaxed pace which allows them to absorb the unfolding sights and sounds of the landscapes they are gliding past. A cruise along the Rhine or the Nile is a journey through history and one that everyone can relive as their vessel plies ancient waterways once used by civilisations far removed from 20th-century cars and planes. And when a cruise ship moors at an exotic island, its passengers are reliving the exhilaration felt by seafarers of old who eagerly anticipated landing at these fragrant shores.

Frequent cruisers tend to be well travelled and interested in a wide range of holidays. They look upon a cruise as not only a complete holiday in itself, but as an opportunity to check out unfamiliar destinations before deciding to book, at some point in the future, a land-based holiday at a particular location. A day in port is an ideal way for travellers to take a good look at a new place with a view to returning at a later date for a longer stay. This sampling of ports is a favourite pastime of cruise passengers who enjoy sharing and comparing their impressions when they return to the ship at the end of the day.

Variety of destinations and types of cruises

Cruises now cover virtually every travel region of the world. Whether it be the ever-popular cruising grounds of the Caribbean and Mediterranean, the distant shores of Alaska and the South Pacific, or the great rivers that meander across continents, wherever there's water there are cruise vessels.

The choice of itineraries and cruises is now very extensive, but an experienced travel agent will save most customers a great deal of time by helping them choose a cruise holiday that will satisfy their individual interests, tastes and expectations.

The Caribbean remains the most popular cruising area with British holidaymakers, and for good reason. Transatlantic airfares have never been cheaper and the Caribbean offers beautiful beaches, sunny weather and historic ports of call where visitors enjoy a unique cultural blend of European colonialism and African heritage.

The Mediterranean is another region which offers cruise visitors a taste of foreign cultures and the opportunity to see some of the world's most famous historical sites – all this against a backdrop of beaches and blue skies. The sunny Med is second only to the Caribbean in terms of popularity with British cruisers, who can choose from a wide selection of fly/cruises or round-trip cruises from the UK.

Quite different in appeal is the rugged grandeur of Alaska, where massive tidewater glaciers and marine mammals such as whales, dolphins and sea otters can be seen from the ship. The Far East is also enticing cruise passengers in ever increasing numbers, while the fjords of Scandinavia remain for many one of the most breathtaking areas to visit by ship.

Whether visiting the famous port cities of the Baltic Sea, passing through the Panama Canal or succumbing to the lure of the South Pacific – the choices are tantalising. And where the ocean ends, river vessels take over with their fascinating voyages along such historic and scenic routes as the Rhine, Main and Danube Rivers of Europe, the Nile of Egypt and America's mighty Mississippi.

Another way to see more of a region is to extend an ocean cruise with an overland tour, such as Alaska's land packages which can include plying the Yukon River on board a paddleboat or taking a private railcar to Denali National Park to view North America's highest peak – Mt McKinley. Another overland tour, for passengers taking an Alaska cruise out of Vancouver, is a coach tour or rail journey to the Canadian Rockies, location of Banff and Jasper National Parks – famous worldwide for their alpine splendour.

A Mediterranean cruise vacation can be extended by boarding the Orient Express in Venice and returning to London by luxury train. A

Caribbean cruise can include, for instance, a pre-or-post land tour of Florida's major attractions or a week-long mid-cruise stay at a resort on the lush island of St Lucia. Cruise travellers to the Far East often disembark for overland tours to Beijing and the Great Wall, and those cruising Australia frequently include an overland trip to the Outback.

Potential cruise holidaymakers must ask themselves not only where they want to go cruising, but on what type of cruise and what type of ship. Will it be a four-day cruise, a one-week cruise, a ten-day cruise, or a round-the world voyage (or a shorter part of one? Will it be a round-trip cruise, a line voyage, a fly/cruise package or possibly a repositioning cruise? Will it be on a classic ocean liner such as the *QE2*, a modern cruise liner like the *Oriana*, a new megaship like the *Sun Princess*, an expedition ship, a tall ship, a small luxury ship or a river vessel? (Refer to the Glossary for an explanation of these terms.)

The Caribbean, for example, can be enjoyed on any type of ship – from the dazzling new megaships that hold up to 2000 passengers to the small sailing ships that anchor off secluded beaches for picnic lunches. The Mediterranean is also served by a complete range of cruise vessels – from modern luxury liners to intimate yacht-like ships – with passengers disembarking at sun-drenched islands and historic ports to view ancient ruins and man-made wonders. And Alaska's lofty scenery can be seen both from the decks of a large cruise ship or amid the casual atmosphere of an expedition vessel carrying less than 200 passengers.

In choosing a ship, it must also be noted that each has its own atmosphere in terms of the nationality of the passengers and crew; the degree of formality or casualness; its specific appeal to singles, families or couples; and its emphasis on certain activities and interests. (Descriptions of specific cruise lines, their ships and itineraries are provided in detail in Chapter 5 of this book.)

Shore activities

As a cruise passenger, your every whim and need will be taken care of, leaving you relaxed and carefree to enjoy the ports of call included in your cruise itinerary. Most passengers eagerly participate in all kinds of shore activities which include sightseeing, shopping, visiting local attractions and places of cultural interest, sunbathing at the beach and engaging in sports.

Most cruise lines offer organised shore excursions for their passengers and these are usually described in a booklet that is enclosed with your cruise tickets as well as at on-board presentations given by the ship's shore excursion manager. There is a charge for such excursions but they are usually fairly priced and the tour operators used are reliable and monitored by the cruise company to ensure they maintain the level of service promised to their passengers.

However, independent-minded passengers need not feel that pre-booked shore excursions are their only option when exploring various ports of call. Choices include renting a car, hiring a taxi, using the public transport system or simply setting off on foot to explore the town and outlying area. With a bit of preparatory reading on the local sights and a reliable map in hand, passengers can see and do a great deal in the time available.

The locale determines the nature of shoreside activities available to cruise passengers. In the Caribbean, for instance, many of the 'shore' activities actually take place in the water – swimming off beaches, snorkelling among coral reefs, scuba diving to shipwrecks now inhabited by tropical fish, and skimming across the water on a windsurfer, catamaran or 12-metre racing yacht. For those who prefer to stay dry, submarine rides and glass bottom boats afford them effortless views of the colourful underwater world.

Airborne excursions include helicopter and seaplane flights for panoramic views of coral atolls and the lush vegetation of island interiors. There are also boat trips to beautiful, secluded beaches and river rafting expeditions through tropical rainforests where waterfalls and freshwater pools create a Garden of Eden setting for the exotic birds, plants and animals living there.

In addition to the Caribbean's natural beauty, its colonial history can be explored on island drives to such points of interest as Nelson's Dockyard on Antigua, Drake's Seat on St Thomas and the imposing fortress of El Morro at San Juan, Puerto Rico. Many of the former plantation estates are open to the public, their grand mansions now museums and the grounds now parkland containing picnic tables and botanical gardens. And of course there are the port cities, where European colonial architecture is reflected in government buildings and grand hotels, and where narrow cobblestone streets are lined with inviting shops and restaurants.

The Mediterranean also offers an appealing combination of beautiful beaches, historic sites and cosmopolitan ports of call where visitors can experience foreign cultures and cuisine. Organised shore excursions are usually coach tours to ancient ruins and temples, monasteries and cathedrals, museums and art galleries, or perhaps a drive into the hills, past cypress trees, olive groves and vineyards, to visit some of the local villages.

Other Mediterranean excursions involve boarding a smaller cruise vessel that takes you to nearby islands to enjoy their coastal scenery, including craggy coves and beach-lined bays. An example of this is the popular ferry ride from Sorrento to the beautiful, cliff-edged island of Capri. For those who prefer to stroll the streets and browse in the local shops, a day in port can soon slip by. Another popular pastime is to simply while away the day at the beach – sunbathing, swimming and gazing out to sea from the shade of a beach umbrella, a cool refreshing drink in hand.

Alaska has some of the most developed and diverse shore excursions of any cruising area. Most people travel to Alaska to see its famed wilderness, which is why side-trips to glaciers, fjords and mountain lakes are extremely popular. Floatplanes and helicopters whisk passengers over glacier-filled valleys and rugged mountains. They fly low enough for passengers to see mountain goats and other wildlife such as beachcombing bears. More wildlife – especially whales and sea otters – can also be spotted on boating and kayaking excursions.

2 What type of cruise? What type of ship?

There's no longer such a thing as a typical cruise. With cruise holidays steadily increasing in popularity, the selection of cruises is also steadily increasing. Today there's a package that appeals to every type of traveller. And the variety of ships now servicing the world's cruising regions is nothing short of stunning. The choices to customers are limited only by each passenger's preference.

Where to go?

The world is broken into cruising regions by the cruise lines. These boundaries sometimes overlap and longer cruises will often encompass a number of regions. Nonetheless, the major areas are the Caribbean, the Mediterranean, Scandinavia and the Baltic, Alaska, trans-Panama Canal, Mexico West, Bermuda, the South Pacific, the Far East, Hawaii and transatlantic cruising.

British cruise travellers – who rank second in the world in terms of numbers – favour the Caribbean first as a destination, followed by the Mediterranean. Also increasing in popularity are cruises to Alaska. The Far East is starting to attract cruise travellers in growing numbers, while Scandinavia and the Baltic continue to attract a sizeable number of cruise visitors each summer.

River cruises are a specialised type of cruise with a strong following among the British, especially itineraries that feature the Nile or the famous rivers of Europe, such as the Rhine and the Danube.

The type of vessel you choose to travel on will of course colour your perceptions of any cruise area, but the scenery, history and local culture of each region will be the same for all passengers. The following is an overview of each major cruise area. (For more detail on ports of call, see Chapter 4.)

The Caribbean

The Caribbean has long appealed to holidaymakers longing to escape the grip of winter for a week or two of sunshine and sandy beaches. And with dozens of islands to visit, a person could return to the Caribbean for numerous visits and still find reasons to come back again.

During the peak cruising season (mid-December to mid-April) some ports of call are thronged with visitors, but the Caribbean Sea is a large body of water and the many ships plying these warm waters spread out and offer varied routes and combinations of ports. The cruise lines are well aware it's the Caribbean's diversity that makes it such an appealing holiday area, which is why their itineraries are arranged to give passengers the best of everything. Careful research and planning goes into choosing ports of call, examples being San Juan for Spanish history and nightlife; St Maarten for Dutch culture and St Martin for French; St Thomas for duty free shopping; St Lucia for lush, mountainous scenery; and Barbados for British heritage.

Of course it's the natural beauty of these tropical islands, their beach-ringed shores lapped by a turquoise sea, that draws visitors from colder climes. In fact, some cruise ships anchor off private undeveloped islands and treat their passengers to a day spent in a classic tropical-island setting. With almost no tidal range in the Caribbean, its waters remain clear and warm all year round – ideal conditions for swimming, snorkelling and other watersports.

The West Indies (also called the Antilles) extend in a wide, 2500-mile arc from Florida to Venezuela, separating the Atlantic Ocean from the Caribbean Sea. Because of its extensive size, the Caribbean has been divided into service areas by the cruise lines. The majority of cruises depart from the Florida ports of Miami or Fort Lauderdale, or from San Juan, Puerto Rico. An Eastern Caribbean cruise will include such destinations as Nassau in the Bahamas, San Juan and the Virgin Islands. Western Caribbean cruises take in Jamaica, Grand Cayman and the Mexican ports of Playa del Carmen and Cozumel. Southern Caribbean cruises sail to the Leeward and Windward groups of the Lesser Antilles as well as such islands as Barbados, Aruba, Curacao and the South American ports of La Guaira (Caracas) and Cartagena.

Caribbean cruises generally range from one to two weeks in length, depending on the area covered, and some itineraries include a partial transit of the Panama Canal. Short three- or four-day cruises out of Miami to the Bahamas are also popular. English is widely spoken throughout the Caribbean, of course.

The Mediterranean

Whether you have a fascination with ancient times or a thoroughly modern interest in diverse cultures, the Mediterranean is for you. It offers dozens of foreign ports located on three different continents and a history dating to the earliest days of antiquity. The world's largest inland sea, the Mediterranean is surrounded by Europe, Asia and Africa. Its coastal regions and islands, graced with fine beaches, offer visitors a climate that is warm and dry with an abundance of sunshine.

The summer season is the most popular time of year for cruising this 'sea in the midst of lands' but cruise ships ply these tide-free waters from spring until the end of autumn. The Mediterranean's mountainous shores, formed over time by earthquakes and volcanic disturbances, are comprised of capes and headlands where clifftop towns and ancient ruins stand.

The varying itineraries offered by the cruise lines are a study in history, art and culture. Rome and Venice contain some of the world's most prized Renaissance art and architecture, and at Istanbul masterpieces of Byzantine architecture can be viewed. The sites of ancient Greece can be revisited on a cruise that stops at Athens to view the Parthenon on the Acropolis, the island of Rhodes (a centre of learning in the 3rd century BC) and the ancient island of Crete, where an advanced civilisation flourished as far back as 3000 BC. Whatever the period, there are suitable ports of call to fascinate the history buff.

In addition to ancient ruins, medieval architecture and Renaissance art, there is the outstanding natural beauty of this region where terraced orchards and vineyards grace the mountainsides and white beaches ring the shorelines. The sea itself is filled with some 400 species of fish, and the sponge and coral life is plentiful. Travellers wishing to sample the Mediterranean's modern-day cultures can stroll round the bazaars and linger at pavement cafés while sampling the local wine and drinking in the surrounding ambiance at each port of call.

Alaska

Spectacular scenery and abundant wildlife are the main attractions of Alaska cruises, which run from early May to late September. The home port for Alaska cruising is Vancouver, Canada, located at the southern end of the Inside Passage – a long and protected stretch of water consisting of hundreds of forested islands, narrow channels and mountain fjords. Much can be seen from the ship's rail en route to the various ports, including hanging waterfalls and tidewater glaciers that drop their ice straight into the sea.

The chance to sight a whale or dolphin adds an additional air of excitement, especially when someone in the dining room shouts 'Whale!' and people abandon their gourmet meals to rush to the windows. Even ports of call are rich in wildlife. Eagles perch on hydro poles and local 'flightseeing' trips whisk passengers over mountains and valleys still blanketed by glaciers that first formed during the last Ice Age. At lower elevations, the mild maritime climate has produced lush forests of spruce, hemlock and cedar, from which the native Indians carve their monumental totem poles.

An Inside Passage cruise to Alaska begins and ends in Vancouver, while cruises that include the Gulf of Alaska in their itinerary operate one-way routes between Vancouver and Anchorage – Alaska's largest city with a population of approximately a quarter of a million. These straight-line cruises are referred to as the 'Glacier Route' because they include some of Alaska's most impressive tidewater glaciers, such as Hubbard Glacier in Yakutat Bay and Columbia Glacier in Prince William Sound.

The Far East

Shrouded in mystery and ancient rituals, the Far East is slowly opening its doors to tourism and visitors can now look inside temples and palaces where philosphers and emperors of ancient dynasties once lived. Hong Kong has long welcomed foreigners and today this free port is the hub of trade, banking and shopping for the Far East. It is also a popular port of call with cruise passengers who enjoy the vibrant pace of this British colony. Hong Kong is being promoted by both local and Chinese tourism officials as a cruise destination that will continue to welcome visitors long after Great Britain's lease expires in 1997.

The exotic ports of south-east Asia are also attracting cruise visitors, places such as the mystical island of Bali, the bustling port of Singapore and the kingdom of Thailand. Another popular cruise destination is Japan, a modern nation of skyscrapers, shops and restaurants but also one of Shinto temples, meditative shrines and bonsai gardens.

Passengers can fly to a local port of south-east Asia or the Far East and embark on a one-to-four-week cruise of the area.

Scandinavia and the Baltic

The fjords of Norway continue to draw visitors each summer. Towering peaks, green mountain valleys, fishing villages nestling at the head of river-fed fjords – this land of endless summer days is breathtakingly beautiful. Its grandeur inspired Edvard Grieg, the 'Voice of Norway', to compose his stirring piano concertos and set the words of Norwegian poets to music. Less than 4% of Norway's rugged land is cultivated, its vast mountain pastures being used for grazing cattle and sheep or, in the north, for raising reindeer.

A Scandinavian cruise also includes the neighbouring countries of Denmark and Sweden. Denmark's cosmopolitan capital of Copen-

hagen contains the Tivoli Gardens and nearby is Elsinore Castle, the setting of Shakespeare's Hamlet. The Swedish capital of Stockholm, situated on several peninsulas and islands, always fascinates visitors with
its Royal Palace and medieval quarter, where winding lanes and arches
lead to restaurants housed in cellars.

Baltic ports of call include Helsinki (capital of Finland) and St
Petersburg, where the Czars of Russia once ruled from the Winter
Palace and where the Hermitage Museum contains some of the world's
greatest works of art.

The Atlantic islands

The Canary Islands, which lie in the Atlantic Ocean off Africa's Spanish
Sahara, once attracted pirates and privateers (Sir Francis Drake among
them) to their beach-lined shores. Today these rugged islands, volcanic
in origin, are a year-round holiday destination with a sub-tropical climate and Spanish flavour. The Madeira Islands, lying 350 miles off
Morocco, are also popular with cruise holidaymakers. Their unusual
scenic beauty, which so captivated Winston Churchill, consists of
mountain peaks, deep green valleys and cliff-lined shores, tempered by
a delightful climate.

Cruises to these island groups often include stops at the African mainland to visit the Moroccan ports of Tangier, Agadir (the 'Miami of
Morocco') and Casablanca with its beguiling blend of Arab bazaars
and stately boulevards from the days of French colonialism.

Transatlantic

Until the development of jet travel, the North Atlantic served as a con-
veyor belt for ships delivering passengers between Europe and North
America. These passengers ranged from the rich and famous who
sailed in luxury with servants, lap dogs and trunks of clothes, to immi-
grants who could afford only the basic accommodation of steerage
class.

Up to the mid-1960s, it was cheaper to cross the Atlantic by ship than by plane. This soon changed, however, especially with the introduction of jumbo jets in the early 1970s. Today, only one major superliner offers regular transatlantic service – the *Queen Elizabeth II*. The most famous cruise ship in the world, Cunard's *QE2* embarks on about two dozen annual sailings between Southampton and New York. Passengers spend five nights on board on a typical crossing and can opt for the air/sea fare which includes a connecting or return flight with British Airways.

Some people book passage on the *QE2* when they are moving across the Atlantic and, in addition to a generous baggage allowance, the *QE2* can transport cars and accommodate pets in its kennel.

Other cruise lines offer seasonal transatlantic crossings – each spring and autumn – when some of their ships travel between the Caribbean and Europe.

Bermuda

Lying some 570 miles off the coast of North Carolina, Bermuda is a bit of 'Olde England' in a semi-tropical setting. Spanish mariners were probably the first explorers to stumble across Bermuda in the 16th century, but the islands remained uninhabited until some British colonists bound for Virginia were shipwrecked there in 1609. Bermuda has remained a British crown colony and thirsty visitors can order a pint in one of the authentic English pubs or watch a local cricket match.

Bermuda pleases all the senses with its fragrant flowers, warm weather, pink coral beaches and pastel-coloured homes. Noel Coward and Mark Twain both wrote effusively about its refined beauty – all contained in an area covering just 21 square miles. Only two miles across at its widest point, Bermuda has over a hundred beaches and eight golf courses, the most golf per acre of anywhere in the world.

From May until October a limited number of cruise lines offer one-week round-trip cruises from New York or Boston. During an average four-day stay at Bermuda, the ship serves as a floating hotel while its passengers tour this enchanting chain of British-flavoured islands.

North America's eastern seaboard

Originally colonised by European settlers, the Atlantic coastlines of Canada and the US are being discovered anew by shipboard passengers who enjoy splendid scenery combined with Old World charm. The region's enduring architecture, regional dialects and local customs all reflect its deep-rooted ties to Europe which hark back to the 16th century with the arrival of Spanish, French, British and Dutch explorers.

Summer and autumn are the seasons for cruising this region of fishing harbours and clapboard houses, Cape Cod mansions and clam chowder soup. Fall foliage cruises are especially popular, when autumn's blaze of colour turns leafy lanes into Norman Rockwell paintings. Specific areas covered by various one-to-two-week cruises include the St Lawrence River, Canada's Atlantic provinces and the American states of New England.

Hawaii and the South Pacific

Most world travellers dream of one day visiting the far-flung islands of the South Pacific. Ever since the fragrant beauty of Tahiti inspired a mutiny among the *Bounty*'s crew, people have been drawn to the South Seas to see what all the fuss was about. Over the years, writers, painters and hedonists have all made the pilgrimage, traditionally arriving by ship and more recently by jet plane.

Today we've come full circle, with cruise lines offering exotic sea voyages to these lagoon-fringed islands of hibiscus and coconut palms. One memorable landfall after another awaits passengers who board a cruise ship bound for the turquoise waters of the South Pacific. San Francisco and Los Angeles are the main ports for these paradise-bound ships, and Hawaii is often the first port of call.

A full cruise of the Pacific, which may also include Australia, New Zealand, south-east Asia and the Far East, will take anywhere from 30 to 100 days depending on the itinerary. However, two-to-three-week segments of these 'grand voyages' can also be booked, with passengers flying to a port of embarkation and flying home from their port of disembarkation. For example, a person could board P & O's *Oriana* in San Francisco for a 19-day cruise through the South Pacific to Sydney, Australia. Or, alternatively, passengers could board the *Canberra* in Sydney for a Pacific cruise to San Francisco.

Mexico's west coast

The golden beaches of Mexico's Pacific coast attract holidaymakers throughout the year, but October to May are the most popular months for cruising. Dubbed the Mexican Riviera, this 2000-mile-long coast of rocky headlands and secluded beaches is famous both for its rugged beauty and its bustling resorts. Each spring and autumn, a fleet of ships travelling between the Caribbean and Alaska offer cruises of the Mexican Riviera.

A number of cruise lines incorporate the Mexican Riviera in their Panama Canal cruises, while others devote entire five-to-ten-day itineraries to the various ports of call situated along this unique stretch of ocean coast. Best known is Acapulco, a resort city situated on a beautiful bay backed by mountains and filled with luxury hotels and private villas, including one at which John and Jackie Kennedy spent their honeymoon.

The Panama Canal

Most seasoned cruisers will agree that travelling along the Panama Canal is something everyone should do at least once in their lifetime. One of the world's great engineering feats, the Panama Canal is a 51-mile-long ditch that was built by the US military to bisect the Isthmus of Panama and thus provide a convenient shipping route between the Atlantic Ocean (via the Caribbean Sea) and the Pacific Ocean. The canal is now a popular itinerary for cruise ships, which regularly pass through its six locks and two lakes. Many of these ships are travelling between Alaska and the Caribbean each spring and autumn. Other ships offer special trans-canal itineraries throughout the winter cruise season. A trans-canal cruise can vary in length from 7 to 17 days. The itineraries offered range from a partial transit of the canal to cruises that include Mexico's Pacific coast and islands of the Caribbean.

River cruises

Rivers were the lifeblood of past civilisations and today they offer cruise travellers a special type of holiday – a journey through history while enjoying the scenic beauty of these magnificent, meandering waterways. In sleek river vessels equipped with expansive viewing lounges and comfortable cabins, passengers can travel the great rivers of Europe and stop at famous cities and towns that were once – and sometimes still are – seats of power and centres of commerce.

The Rhine, principal river of Europe, rises in the Swiss Alps and flows through Switzerland, Liechtenstein, Austria, Germany, France and the Netherlands before emptying into the North Sea. A river cruise along this historic trade route is one through breathtaking gorges and past terraced vineyards and medieval castles perched on historically strategic banks. The Romans first established forts and colonies along its western banks, followed by robber barons of the Middle Ages who built castles along this important trade artery and exacted heavy tolls from passing ships and barges.

A Rhine cruise usually begins or ends in Amsterdam, where narrow canal houses line the bicycle-clogged streets and stone bridges span the city's network of canals. At nearby Arnhem you board your river vessel and begin the voyage among the tulip fields and windmills of Holland before joining the Lower Rhine. Guest lecturers, experts in such fields as medieval history and European architecture, will be on board to illuminate the passing sights as well as the historic towns and cities included in the cruise itinerary.

The Danube, less busy than the Rhine, rises from two sources in Germany's Black Forest and flows into Austria, past Linz and Vienna, then skirts Hungary before turning to flow across its central region to Budapest. A whole day is usually spent in Vienna, for centuries one of the great cities of Europe and today a fascinating place for visitors interested in art, music, architecture and those delicious pastries served at its famous coffee houses.

Other river cruises take place on the scenic Elbe, which begins in the mountains of the old Kingdom of Bohemia; the Main, which connects the Rhine and Danube via the Main–Danube Canal; the Moselle, a tributary of the Rhine which twists and turns its way south past German castles, vineyards and riverside villages; the romantic Rhône, which wends its way through France's beautiful Burgundy and Beaujolais wine regions; and the Seine, flowing through the heart of Paris and the countryside of Normandy, where Monet and other French artists were inspired by the green and rolling landscapes.

The ancient civilisation of the Nile can also be explored on a river cruise. The Nile – 'long river between the deserts' – is the heart of one of mankind's earliest settlements. History here is measured not in centuries but in millennia. The Age of the Great Pyramids was 2680–2565 BC and the ones located near modern-day Cairo are the largest and finest of their kind. Other monumental forms of architecture include great temples, their massive facades flanked by sloping towers and their entrances approached between rows of sculptured sphinxes.

River cruises in other parts of the world include North America's popular Mississippi riverboats, their steam engines driving both a huge paddlewheel on the stern and a pipe-organ on deck. These river cruises are a trip back in time as passengers gaze at the passing sights of Mark Twain's beloved Mississippi while listening to Dixieland jazz and sipping mint juleps.

What length of cruise?

Once you have decided where you would like to go on a cruise, the next step is deciding its length. For the first-time cruiser, a short three-to-seven-day cruise is perhaps the best choice. This gives a person a taste of what cruising is like without committing a great deal of time and money to a new type of holiday. Also, because cruise fares are generally calculated on a per-day basis, you won't be paying a premium for taking a short versus a long cruise .

Cunard's introductory cruises on the famous *QE2* include such itineraries as an Autumn Party Cruise in which passengers embark at

Above *The best known 'classic' liner,*
Cunard's Queen Elizabeth II (QE2).
Left *Carnival Cruise Lines'* Tropicale *typifies*
the modern 'megaship' design.

Opposite Princess Cruises' Royal Princess *is a fine example of the 1980s generation of cruise ships.* **Above** *The river cruiser* Royal Rhapsody, *one of several vessels in Thomas Cook Holidays' Nile fleet.*

The more adventurous side of cruising is represented by expedition ships like Spirit of Alaska, *seen above off the coast of British Columbia, and sailing vessels such as* Windsong, *pictured below in the waters of French Polynesia.*

Southampton on a Friday evening to spend a weekend enjoying the facilities of this 'City at Sea'. A slightly longer cruise of four nights is offered in early December, departing Southampton for a day in Le Havre and another day in Amsterdam before returning to England. P & O also offers an autumn cruise of three nights, round trip, on board the *Canberra* departing from Southampton for the Normandy ports of Le Havre and Cherbourg.

CTC Cruise Lines offers a number of six-to-eight-night round-trip cruises well suited to first-time cruisers, who can choose from a Scandinavian cruise out of London or Edinburgh, or a cruise to France, Spain and Portugal out of Bristol. The *QE2* also sails to Scandinavia and to the Canary Islands and Madeira; these are eight-night round-trip cruises out of Southampton.

First-time cruisers needn't restrict their choice of itinerary to those departing the UK. With air travel providing quick access to every cruising area in the world, it has become increasingly convenient for passengers to fly to their port of embarkation by booking an air/cruise package.

The Caribbean offers some of the best fly/cruise options for UK passengers. Royal Caribbean Cruise Lines, for example, has a wide range of itineraries starting with three-and-four-night cruises out of Miami to the Bahamas, as does Carnival Cruise Lines. For UK holidaymakers already planning a trip to Florida, it's easy to include a short Bahamian cruise in their travel agenda.

This kind of cruise is also a possibility for those travelling to other parts of North America. Throughout the summer and autumn, New York is the base port for seven-day cruises to Bermuda, and Montreal is the base port for round-trip cruises of the St Lawrence and Canada's Atlantic seaboard. Visitors to Western Canada may want to combine a trip to the Canadian Rockies with a round-trip cruise out of Vancouver to Alaska. These seven-day cruises of the Inside Passage are spent along the mountainous channels and forested fjords of British Columbia and Alaska.

Of course some people may decide that, first cruise or not, they would rather opt for a longer itinerary. As long as you have chosen a ship that suits your tastes, you will not regret this decision. In fact, many people who take a seven-day cruise will say afterwards they didn't want to get off the ship at the end of the trip. By then they had become familiar with the ship and, having quite naturally fallen into a rhythm of shipboard life which they were enjoying, could quite happily have continued the cruise for another week or so.

Pick the number of days you would like to spend on a cruise and there will probably be an itinerary of that length. Whether you opt for an eight-day round trip from the UK or a round-the-world journey of 90 days or more, there's bound to be a cruise that fits into your schedule.

Which ship?

Although every ship has its own personality, it is helpful to know the general category to which it belongs. The following section is designed to explain the different categories and some of the criteria that should be taken into consideration when deciding which cruise vessel would best suit *your* personality and travel budget.

Classic liners

These ships were built between 1950 and 1969, when transatlantic crossings were still a major mode of transport not yet eclipsed by jet travel. Designed for the rigours of an ocean crossing, the classic liners were long and sleek with heavy riveted plating, deep keels and sheltered deck space to shield passengers from inclement weather. The cabins tend to be roomy with plenty of wardrobe space, especially those in the former first-class sections of the ship, but the corridors are generally narrower than those of modern ships. Public areas evoke an atmosphere of tradition and refinement, with such features as grand staircases and original wood panelling, brass fixtures and stained glass. Public rooms in those days were actually set aside for smoking and featured leather-lined walls to absorb the smoke.

The *QE2* was the last of the classic liners to be launched (in 1969). Other classic liners still in service are the *Canberra* (launched in 1961), the *Norway* (launched as the *France* in 1960) and the *Rotterdam* (launched in 1959). P & O's *Canberra*, an enduring favourite with British cruisers, was refurbished in 1992 and sails the Mediterranean, Iberia, the Caribbean and around the world. Norwegian Cruise Lines' *Norway*, which underwent a multi-million-dollar conversion in 1979–80, is dedicated to Caribbean waters all year round. The *Rotterdam*, Holland America's flagship, embarks on Alaska cruises each summer and a variety of itineraries during the rest of the year. And Cunard's *QE2* – extensively refurbished in 1987 and again in late 1994 – provides regular transatlantic crossings as well as holidays to a wide variety of the world's cruising areas.

Modern cruise liners

The early 1980s marked a turning point in the cruise industry. As more and more people discovered the merits of a cruise holiday, the demand for additional ships began to surge. This new breed of ship was designed not for long ocean voyages but for coastal cruising and island-hopping. In between ports of call, passengers of the 80s wanted – and got – plenty of diversions. Thus the new ships were dubbed 'floating resorts' because of their large outdoor decks, swimming pools, show lounges and casinos. Cabins were fitted with picture windows instead of portholes, some even with sliding glass doors that opened onto private verandahs.

Traditionalists decried the boxy look of these new ships, as well as the fact that cabins were generally smaller than on the classic liners. The rationale behind smaller cabin space was that passengers now spent far more time in the public areas and at the various ports of call than they did in their cabins. The new liners were one-class ships, with every passenger enjoying access to all of the ship's lavish public areas.

Some trademark ships of the 1980s are Royal Caribbean Cruise Line's *Song of America*, Princess Cruises' *Royal Princess* and Holland America's *Nieuw Amsterdam* and *Noordam* (sister ships). They remain outstanding ships, in no way overshadowed by the newer ships, for they offer many passengers a satisfying balance of facilities and size.

Megaships

While the new ships of the 80's were built to accommodate from 500 to 1500 passengers, the megaships of the 90's are being designed to carry between 1500 and 2500 passengers. Their superstructures are similar to the 80s cruise liner, but on a larger scale. Towering a dozen or more storeys high and topped with extensive sun and sports decks, these megaships are more than floating resorts – they are floating holiday communities.

Royal Caribbean Cruise Line's new *Legend of the Seas* has a golf course on its upper deck and Princess Cruises' *Sun Princess* (entering service in December, 1995) is 14 storeys high, contains five swimming pools and requires a full-time gardener to tend the ship's lushly landscaped interior.

Luxury small ships

In contrast to the megaships are the intimate luxury ships carrying 100 to 300 passengers. Being aboard one of these upmarket vessels is similar to being on board a billionaire's private yacht. The service is attentive and personalised, and the ships can pull into smaller ports than their larger cousins. The on-board facilities are of course not as extensive as on the large liners, but all appointments are of the highest quality and some of the features are unique, such as a stern that folds out into a swimming platform from which passengers can take part in various water sports while the ship is at anchor. Cunard's *Sea Goddess I* and *II* are examples of luxury small ships.

Expedition ships

These ships have a casual atmosphere with the emphasis on learning about the areas being explored. Guest lecturers, slide-shows and well-stocked reference libraries are standard features. Those vessels with shallow draughts can pull into small ports and remote anchorages where passengers are taxied ashore in rubber landing craft. The larger ships usually have reinforced hulls for cruising the polar regions. The chance to observe wildlife in a pristine setting is a major appeal of these types of cruise vessel, which are popular in Alaska and other remote wilderness areas. These include the luxury Windstar vessels and the ships of Windjammer Barefoot Cruises.

Sailing vessels ('tall ships')

The romance of sail is captured in sail-powered cruise vessels ranging from small windjammers to large clipper-style ships carrying a few hundred passengers. While all have an engine on board to help propel the vessel under certain conditions, the sails are raised much of the time and passengers are often encouraged to get involved in their handling through informal sailing classes. Life on board these vessels is unstructured and, when at anchor, passenger activities usually include beach picnics and watersports. Cabins are often modest and meals less elaborate than on a cruise liner. Sail-powered cruise vessels are popular in the Caribbean and South Pacific.

River cruise vessels

Carrying up to a hundred passengers, these long sleek vessels are custom-designed for river cruising. Facilities may include a small health club and theatre but more often consist of an upper-deck swimming pool, whirlpool and canopied deck chair area for those who prefer sitting in the shade as their vessel glides past scenic shores. An enclosed viewing lounge with large windows provides a comfortable vantage point for observing the passing sights, their historical background provided by onboard lecturers who are experts in their academic fields. Cabins range from comfortable to spacious and the dining room is usually intimate and elegant.

The vessel remains docked overnight, travelling only during daylight hours. The itinerary is what's important to a passenger booking a river cruise, so the emphasis is less on facilities and activities than on a refined holiday for those who appreciate and want to learn more about the history and culture of the area.

The Thomas Cook Nile fleet, built specifically for cruise tours of Egypt, contains prime examples of this type of vessel.

Determining a ship's atmosphere

They say a 'happy ship' is one with a happy crew. It might be added that this also applies to the passengers. And no passenger is happy unless he or she feels comfortable with a particular ship's atmosphere. There are a number of factors that determine each ship's prevailing atmosphere and these include the ship's size, its rating (i.e. level of accommodation and service), and the age group it attracts.

Ships are measured in gross registered tons and the higher the tonnage, the larger the ship in terms of total on-board space. The new megaships are not necessarily longer or wider than their predecessors but they have a taller superstructure (ie. more decks) which is reflected in their high tonnage measurements of over 70,000 tons.

Ships are 'rated' on a wide range of criteria, but some of the basic ones to keep in mind are the passenger/space ratio and the crew/passenger ratio. The first will help you determine the amount of space each passenger has on board. For instance, a ratio of 40+ is the ultimate in spaciousness, 20–30 is moderately spacious, and 10 is high density. The ratio of crew to passengers will determine the level of service. On luxury vessels, there are almost as many crew members as passengers, while ships in the mid-range price category generally have a ratio of one crew member for every two-to-three passengers. The ratings system adopted in this book is a broad 'star' rating, similar to that for hotels. ratings run from 3★ to 5★. See Chapter 8 for more details.

A cruise line's brochure will also hold clues to the type of vessel you are considering. Some emphasise their ships' luxury service, while others focus more on the wide range of activities and high level of fun enjoyed by their passengers. Some lines attract a young crowd, others a mature clientele. One ship might be perfect for honeymooners while another is more suitable for families. One ship might appeal to a mature couple seeking quiet refinement and another will be attractive to passengers who like casualness and sports-oriented activities.

A ship's character is also determined by the nationality of its officers and hotel staff, and by the location of its head office. The naval academies of seafaring nations, such as Britain and Norway, produce many of the officers employed by the cruise lines. P & O, for example, has British officers; those running the ships of Royal Caribbean Cruise Lines and Norwegian Cruise Lines are often from Norway. Cunard uses both British and Norwegian officers, and the ships of Holland America Line are commanded by Dutch officers. The nationality of the captain and his crew often set the style of the ship.

The nationality of the hotel staff is another factor to consider. The Hotel Manager and senior service personnel are often of the same nationality as the officers, while those heading various subordinate departments might be from other countries. Many ships have an international staff, so your cabin steward, dining room waiter and bar staff could all be from different countries.

Last but not least is the prevailing nationality of the passengers. Those who want to take a bit of Britain with them when they go cruising are most comfortable on British-based cruise lines, such as Cunard, P & O, CTC and Fred Olsen. The majority of the world's cruise passengers are American, so the majority of cruise lines cater to English-speaking passengers, thus providing UK passengers with the option to choose not only from the British fleet of cruise ships but also from an extensive selection of ships serving the North American market. British staff often work on board these American-oriented ships. (The atmosphere and nationality of each cruise line is described in Chapter 5.)

Types of cruises

Newcomer cruises

A number of cruise lines offer a special package called a Newcomers Cruise to passengers who are booking with them for the first time. For a reasonable fee a first-time passenger receives benefits that vary with each cruise company but often include such enticements as free British Rail travel to the port of embarkation, automatic cabin upgrades, on-board spending money, a complimentary shore excursion and an invitation to a Newcomers Cocktail Party.

Honeymoons and wedding anniversaries

Newlyweds and couples seeking a romantic way to celebrate a special wedding anniversary often choose a cruise. To add to the natural allure of such a holiday, most cruise lines provide a few extras to these special couples. Automatic cabin upgrades and complimentary champagne are just some of the perks they can expect to receive.

Theme and special interest cruises

Theme cruises continue to grow in popularity as people increasingly want to get more out of their holiday than simply lying about on a beach. Many people are finding they enjoy combining a special interest or hobby with a cruise holiday. Relaxed and free of any daily mundane decision making, they can immerse themselves in pastimes they find stimulating and enjoyable. At the end of the holiday, they return home feeling recharged and also savouring a sense of accomplishment for having improved, for instance, their golf skills or their appreciation of classical music.

Both Cunard and P & O offer special interest cruises. Guest lecturers (often celebrity authors) and classical concerts are regularly featured on board the *QE2*. Special themes have included a VE Day Commemoration cruise with stars of the era providing nostalgic entertainment. Opera at Sea is another theme featured on Cunard's upmarket luxury ships.

P & O offers an impressive selection of theme cruises throughout the year on many of its sailings. Special interests include gardening, birdwatching, classical music, photography and dancing – Scottish Highland, English Country, ballroom, Latin, sequence and old time. The guest hosts for these theme cruises include experts such as David Stevens from BBC's 'Gardener's World' and Roger Lovegrove from the RSPB.

Mike Maloney of Mirror Group Newspapers is among the professional photographers who give talks and clinics on selected P & O cruises, and television personality Tony Hart hosts arts and crafts festivals on special sailings. Hosting P & O's classical music festivals, featuring acclaimed musicians, is Richard Baker. Bridge players can book onto cruises that feature a full EBU-licensed congress afloat and gourmets can take a cordon bleu cruise hosted by a master chef.

P & O also offers sports-oriented cruises with instruction in golf and the opportunity to play ashore, football coaching provided by former England players and FA coaches, and cricket matches on board and ashore with coaching provided by former England cricketers. There's even an Antiques Festival held on board selected P & O cruises with experts from BBC's 'Antiques Roadshow' hosting a series of lectures and evaluations.

Expedition and river cruising are theme cruises in themselves, each cruise's theme determined by the region being visited. For instance, an expedition cruise of Alaska will focus on the glaciers, wildlife and nature. A river cruise of the Nile will enlighten its passengers with an archaeological look at ancient Egypt.

Escorted cruises and land tours

Holidaymakers who fly to distant destinations to join a cruise, are often tempted to include some land travel while there. The cruise companies have anticipated this and they offer passengers a wide range of pre-and-post-cruise land tours.

An African land adventure might include a few nights in Cape Town followed by visits to the Cape of Good Hope, wineries, ostrich farms and cheetah ranches. Highlights of an extended Australian cruise include such contrasting settings as the cosmopolitan city of Sydney and the outback town of Alice Springs; the stark sight of Ayers Rock and the thriving submarine life of the Great Barrier Reef.

Passengers cruising the Far East invariably choose to include a visit to Beijing, where the Forbidden City, Summer Palace and nearby Great Wall await those fascinated by this ancient empire. Japan is another cruise destination that lures passengers inland to view its imperial palaces, Buddhist temples and meditative gardens.

Caribbean cruises, many of which use Miami and Fort Lauderdale as their base ports, present a perfect opportunity for passengers to see the sights of Florida before or after their cruise. Orlando's Walt Disney World and Epcot Center, the Everglades National Park and the Florida Keys are all major holiday destinations, as are the beach resorts that line much of the state's coastline.

Mediterranean cruisers can opt for a return trip to England on board the Venice–London Orient Express. And the Canadian Rockies and Denali National Park are popular destinations for cruise passengers looking to extend their Alaska cruise with a land tour.

Whatever part of the world you visit by cruise ship, you can usually extend your stay through land tour packages organised by the cruise line. Overland transport is often a combination of coach, rail and jet travel.

Shipboard activities

The one word cruise lines fear above all else is *boredom*. Even the most humble of ships will make a decent effort to keep its passengers amused and a number of sports and recreational opportunities will be offered by the ship's cruise director (see p. 49) on a daily basis. Not every ship offers all activities we've listed here, but most will offer at least some and it's possible to find out, before booking, which ships offer the activities you consider essential to an enjoyable cruise holiday.

Walking, for example, is popular with everyone, which is why almost all ships have what is called a 'promenade deck' – named from the days when promenade meant a stroll. Now it means anything from a fast walk to a slow jog but its common purpose remains: exercising in the fresh air. Ships with a teak promenade deck are especially delightful to walk on and most promenade decks encircle the entire ship.

Probably the next most common exercise facility is some sort of gym room where those who enjoy a more concentrated regime of activity will be able to work out on equipment or to the directions of a fitness instructor. A swimming pool is another fairly standard feature on modern cruise ships. Beyond this the range of activities offered is quite varied. The size and class of ship will to some extent determine the recreational possibilities, and the lists shown here are not exhaustive.

SHIPBOARD ACTIVITIES

Athletics and physical activities

Walk a Mile on the Promenade Deck

Low-impact aerobics/ High-impact aerobics

Lower back and abdominal exercises

Golf chipping

Men's and ladies' golf putting tournaments

Dance classes

Deck tennis, football and cricket

Volleyball, basketball & table tennis tournaments

Quoits tournaments

Health and beauty

Fashion shows

Hair, beauty and fitness demonstrations

Skin care and cosmetic demonstrations

Slimming, toning and nutrition

Games

Backgammon tournaments

Gin rummy

Duplicate Bridge championships

Blackjack tournaments

International horseracing

Quizzes and panel games

Jackpot bingo

Dominoes, Scrabble and Monopoly

Chess and draughts

Classes and demonstrations

Cooking class with an executive chef

Cheese fondue demonstrations

Vegetable carving and ice carving demonstrations

Napkin folding and flower arranging

Photography tips from the ship's chief photographer

Learn to play blackjack, craps and roulette

Ship tours

Guided tours of various working areas of the ship are conducted by junior officers and members of the ship's staff:

Kitchen

Navigation Bridge

Engine Room

Back Stage

Casino

Art and antiques

---

3 Did you know? Some facts about cruising

Cruising is not prohibitively expensive

Cruising used to be very expensive, but no longer. In real terms, the cost of cruising has been steadily decreasing and it is now one of the most economical holidays available when all daily costs are taken into account. The costs of your accommodation, meals and entertainment are all included in the price of your ticket. Even the airfare – if you have to fly to the port of embarkation – is usually included and regional flights are sometimes complimentary. When you leave home at the beginning of your cruise holiday, you already know exactly what it will cost.

Of course you will probably incur some extra expenses but these are entirely at your discretion. Organised shore excursions, for example, will cost extra, as will personal services such as haircuts and massages on board the ship. Alcoholic drinks ordered in lounges and dining rooms will also be charged to your cabin, as will purchases at the on-board shops. However, a person could theoretically step on board a cruise ship and not spend another penny for the duration of the trip.

How, you might ask, has cruising become so economical? The answer is economy of scale and competitiveness. Many of the cruise companies have built large ships that carry high numbers of passengers, and this increased capacity has allowed them to reduce costs. While some luxury ships still serve an upmarket clientele, the average holidaymaker can now board a cruise ship and enjoy its relaxed ambiance and wide array of facilities for a fraction of what a similar cruise would have cost twenty years ago. And, as more and more people take to cruising – as did more than a quarter of a million British travellers last year – new ships are being added to the current selection. This allows customers to shop around for the cruise best suited to their budget and personal taste. It's a competitive market for the cruise lines and a shopper's paradise for the customer.

Cruises fit into normal holiday periods

Cruising used to appeal mainly to people with lots of leisure time on their hands. Not so today. With jet planes whisking passengers to their ports of embarkation, cruises are now offered in lengths ranging from three days to round-the-world voyages of three months.

Cruises of three-to-four days duration are a good way for first-timers to test the water and see if cruising appeals to them. Highly popular are the one-to-two-week cruises, which fit into most people's holiday schedules. With time at a premium as people juggle their work commitments and personal lives, a one-to-two week cruise is an ideal way to visit a number of destinations in a short period of time yet still feel relaxed and refreshed at the end of the holiday.

Cruising is for all age groups

The average age of cruise passengers is steadily dropping, with almost 40% of new passengers now under the age of 35. Cruising has become a novelty for people who grew up with jet travel and fast-paced lifestyles. They enjoy the relaxed atmosphere of a ship and the freedom to do whatever they choose while on board.

Those who grew up in the Swinging 60s are now leading younger generations across the gangway onto ships where casualness has replaced conformity and fun takes precedence over etiquette. Not that common courtesy has been tossed overboard, but good manners are now practised with a friendly openness.

Young singles, newlyweds, couples with children, empty nesters and retired people all enjoy cruising for different reasons. A cruise holiday can be whatever you want it to be – from slow-paced to action-packed – which is why passengers of all ages enjoy shipboard travel.

Children are often the biggest fans of cruising. They are free of the shadow of their parents, who don't feel the need to check on their youngsters wherever they go. In addition to having fun at the activities organised for them, children enjoy the special treatment they receive from the cruise staff who often dote on their younger passengers. Many children thrive on the attention they receive and respond by behaving like adults in the dining room and other public areas of the ship.

Cruising is not restrictive

A common concern among people contemplating their first cruise, is that the ship will feel too small and claustrophobic. They don't realise how different a cruise ship is from a hotel. Entire decks of large cruise ships are devoted to public areas that include dining rooms, lounges, bars, shops and poolside areas.

A person could actually get lost on some of the larger ships and location maps are placed near stairwells and lifts to help passengers find their way around the ship. Many passengers find it takes a good week on board the ship before they have explored all of its public spaces and can find their way around the entire ship with total ease.

There is no forced sociability on board

Many people who haven't yet cruised envisage a typical cruise as having no end of organised activities in which they must take part. Yes, there is plenty of group activity for those who enjoy meeting people, but there aren't non-stop announcements and cruise employees aren't continually herding reluctant passengers off to the next event. The daily programme, slipped under your cabin door, is what keeps you informed of organised activities and you can ignore any or all of them if you so choose.

Passengers seeking quiet solitude can usually find just that. They can request a table for two in the dining room, rather than a larger table of six or eight people. They can slip into the library or find themselves a quiet viewing lounge or deck chair in which to read and chat quietly with a companion. The outside decks are often surprisingly empty of fellow passengers, depending on the time of day and the ship's location. And of course, passengers can always retire to the privacy of their cabin whenever they like.

The operative word is 'control'. You have complete control of how you spend your time on a cruise holiday.

A trunk of new clothes isn't necessary

Go ahead and buy some new clothes if you like – that's part of the fun of going on holiday – but your wardrobe probably contains everything you need for cruising.

For daytime activities on the ship and in port, casual and comfortable clothes are the norm. You'll want to pack something a bit dressier for semi-formal nights in the dining room, such as a skirt or dress for the ladies and a sports jacket for the men. For the one or two formal evenings on the ship, you will need nothing more special than a cocktail dress for the ladies and a dark suit and and tie for the men. You can, if you like, pack a sequined evening gown or dinner jacket but this is not mandatory.

Passengers are usually required to wear a cover-up over their bathing suits before entering the dining room for lunch or wandering through other indoor areas of the ship. And on casual evenings, jeans, shorts and t-shirts are considered a bit too casual in the dining room.

The ship's daily programme will advise you of each evening's dress code, but this is fairly flexible. However, most passengers do respect the dress code and many enjoy the opportunity to look their best at dinner each night. After all, part of the shipboard dining experience is the elegant atmosphere and attentive service, so why not dress the part?

Everyone cruises 'First Class' today

On today's cruise ships, everyone cruises 'First Class'. All of the ship-board facilities, be it the swimming pool, show theatre, cinema or gymnasium, are open to all passengers regardless of the deck on which their cabin is located. On a few cruise liners the passengers are assigned to specific dining rooms according to their grade of cabin, but all other public areas are accessible to everyone. No one misses out on anything. There is always room in the theatre for those who want to take in that evening's live show and there's no queueing for drinks – these will be brought to your table. Everyone receives the same service and enjoys the same cruise experience regardless of the cabin they booked.

The size and location of cabin is more important to some passengers than to others. Some feel they spend such little time in their cabin, it's unnecessary to pay for something larger. Others enjoy retiring to a stateroom that is more spacious and comfortable than a standard cabin and these people are willing to pay more for their personal accommodation. However, regardless of what you eventually decide regarding a choice of cabin, the rest of the ship is yours to fully enjoy.

Fine dining is still part of the experience

One thing that hasn't changed on board cruise ships is the excep-tional cuisine. Most people embark on a cruise anticipating lavish meals and they are rarely disappointed. With a new lunch and dinner menu presented daily, from which you can order as many courses as you like, a cruise can be an epicurean delight. And there is enough variety in the menu to suit all tastes – from basic to gourmet. However, if nothing on the menu appeals to you, there are always plenty of alternatives.

The meals enjoyed in the course of a cruise could quickly add up to hundreds of pounds if a passenger were paying for them individually at comparable restaurants on shore. Yet, surprisingly, these high-qual-ity and varied meals account for only a fraction of the price a cruise

Whatever the style and atmosphere of the ship, the Hotel Manager and his staff are dedicated to ensuring that all passengers enjoy the best possible standards of accommodation, services and cuisine.

Most of today's cruises do not demand very formal dress. For most of the day dress is casual, and when dining in the evenings it is normal to wear smart, semi-formal clothes.

Relaxation on board a cruise ship can be found in many forms, whether in the solitude of a quiet corner of the deck or in the luxurious surroundings of a solarium such as the one pictured below, on the Legend of the Seas *(Royal Caribbean Cruise Lines)*.

Modern ships vie with one another in the splendour of their public rooms and areas. **Above** The 'Romeo and Juliet' dining room of the Legend of the Seas. **Left** The atrium on the Crystal Symphony *(Crystal Cruises)*

ticket. It's estimated that food generally accounts for 8–9% of a cruise line's total operating costs.

On a ship holding 1200 passengers, there are over 5000 meals prepared each day. A typical kitchen staff on a ship this size consists of the Executive Chef, 11 Chefs de Partie (Department Heads), 12 Aides de Cuisine, four Demi Chefs, 26 assistant cooks, 14 pantry personnel and 26 workers in charge of cleaning the kitchen and clearing up. Provisions for a 7-day cruise might include 8000 lb of beef, 36 lb of caviar, 680 lb of cheese, 465 gallons of ice cream, 25,000 lb of fresh vegetables, 24,000 lb of fresh fruit, 7000 bottles of beer and 1600 bottles of wine.

The role of the cruise staff

No cruise would be half so enjoyable without the remarkable service that passengers receive from the ship's staff. The captain, chief engineer and their officers and crew make up only a small portion of total staff on board a ship. The majority of employees are engaged in transforming the ship into a floating resort. Overseen by the hotel manager, who is second in rank only to the Captain, the hotel staff work in wonderful ways – many of which are invisible to the average passenger.

Most visible to passengers is the cruise director who oversees all the ship's entertainment. He or she usually has a background in show business and brings to the job a level of energy and enthusiasm that is infectious. Outgoing and easy to approach, the cruise director is on hand at all social functions and is master of ceremonies at each evening's stage show. By the end of the cruise, most passengers feel as if they personally know the cruise director.

It's the ability of the cruise director and other staff to make passengers feel completely at ease and free to ask for any type of assistance that keeps repeat cruisers coming back. They work tirelessly to ensure their passengers are having a good time, while maintaining a cheerful disposition at all times.

This also applies to the dining room staff. Dinnertime is especially special on board a ship, with the the maitre d' and his assistants lavishing attention on each passenger who enters the dining room. Waiters politely assist the ladies with their chairs and water glasses are promptly filled. The evening's menu is slipped into each arrival's hands and pre-dinner conversation fills the room, all in anticipation of the delicious meal about to be served.

While passengers are being pampered in the dining room, their cabin stewards are busy tidying and cleaning their rooms for the second time that day. No wonder some people don't want to disembark at the end of their cruise. It's always a bit of a shock to step back into the real world where you no longer enjoy the special status of being a cruise passenger!

Seasickness

When ocean liners regularly crossed the North Atlantic during the first half of this century, it was not unusual for passengers to get seasick – especially if the ship was pitching or rolling in the big seas of a winter storm. Today the majority of cruises take place in protected coastal waters and most passengers experience little if any discomfort on a regular one-to-two-week cruise.

The aim of modern ship travel is no longer to get from one side of an ocean to another but to meander from port to port, so the ship's routes do not generally entail long stretches of open-water sailing. Cruise itineraries are planned to coincide with a region's fair-weather season and accurate forecasting allows a captain to alter his ship's course if bad weather is approaching. Modern cruise ships also have stabilisers – fin-like appendages that can be extended from each side of the ship just below its waterline – that will prevent a ship from rolling excessively in a big sea.

All this being said, some people are susceptible to motion sickness but they needn't suffer in silence while cruising. There are a number of effective remedies at their disposal, including such simple solutions as standing out on deck in the fresh air or nibbling on crackers and sipping ginger ale. Some people find that wearing special wristbands, the balls of which rest on an acupressure point, are all they need to prevent any queasiness. And the purser's office usually stocks tablets that reduce motion sickness and have no side effects. Should a passenger become concerned about their seasickness, medical attention can be sought immediately with the ship's qualified medical personnel. However, motion sickness is rarely a serious problem on most cruises and those who experience it usually find it is short lived.

It doesn't have to be the 'trip of a lifetime'

Many people delay taking a cruise until they have a special reason for doing so. For years they talk about 'one day taking a cruise', possibly to celebrate a milestone – a wedding anniversary or a long-anticipated retirement. Yet, a cruise needn't be considered a once-in-a-lifetime experience.

With today's fly/cruise packages, shorter itineraries and cheaper fares, a cruise holiday can become an annual holiday for those who like to travel. Cruise lines and travel agents value their repeat passengers, often offering them first choice on special packages and generous early-booking discounts. Seasoned passengers, rather than tiring of the experience, usually find that they get more and more out of cruising with each trip they go on. They come to know which cruise lines appeal to their personal tastes and what type of ship they prefer cruising on, and they discover that for them one of the best ways to see the world is from the deck of a ship.

Repeat cruisers are usually well-travelled and enjoy all types of holidays, so they find that cruising fits in well with their other travel experiences. They might, for instance, go on a one-week cruise of the Mediterranean, then return the next year to an island resort they briefly visited while in port. The following year they're off to the Caribbean, cruising to three or four ports of call with a view to possibly returning for a longer, land-based stay at one the islands they visit by ship. Cruising, for many, becomes another mode of travel and adds variety to their holiday choices.

4 Ports of call

This chapter is designed to give you a closer look at the cruising areas that were briefly described in Chapter 2, with highlights of some of the popular ports of call. In some ways it is the heart of the book; the lure of foreign lands is still for many people the prime reason for going on a cruise. Faraway ports, located on different continents, breathing different cultures, are the stuff of wanderlust and romance. The offshore wind, laden with unfamiliar frangrances of blossoms and aromatic wood, is impalpable, enslaving, casting the first impressions of a new land. Sometimes, as Joseph Conrad observed, pulling into port in the early morning has the effect of a charm. like a whispered promise of mystery and delight.

Alaska

Each year Alaska attracts a record number of cruise passengers who come to see this vast and rugged coastline of mountains, forests, glaciers and fjords. From May to October, ships wend their way along the narrow, winding channels of the Inside Passage – so named because it lies within a long chain of coastal islands which act as a buffer from the open waters of the North Pacific. Wildlife sighted along the way can include whales, dolphins, porpoises, sea otters, bears and bald eagles.

The majority of cruise ships trace two popular routes. The Inside Passage route is a round-trip, one-week cruise from Vancouver, Canada; the Glacier Route is a seven-day, line voyage between Vancouver and Anchorage that includes the Inside Passage, Gulf of Alaska and Prince William Sound. An Inside Passage cruise usually includes a close look at some tidewater glaciers, such as those at the head of narrow, cliff-sided Tracy Arm, or those found in the many inlets of Glacier Bay – a body of water that was completely filled with ice as recently as 200 years ago when Britain's George Vancouver sailed past its ice-clogged entrance.

Major ports of the Inside Passage

Ports of call along the Inside Passage are situated on the edge of islands or at the base of coastal mountains, and most are accessible only by water or by air. Wedged between mountains and sea, Alaskan ports have scenic settings and a friendly atmosphere. Their pioneer heritage is illustrated by the wooden warehouses, canneries and boardwalks built on pilings. Native totem poles are on display at various locations. The moist maritime climate of coastal Alaska has produced dense forests of towering evergreens that surround these pockets of habitation. The ports are compact and can easily be explored on foot. Many visitors, while their ship is in port, take excursions to the outlying wilderness areas to view glaciers or spot some wildlife.

Ketchikan, a cannery town founded in the late 1800's, is situated at the mouth of Ketchikan Creek where salmon can be seen swimming upstream as they return to their spawning grounds. The region's vibrant native culture is reflected in numerous totem pole displays. A popular wilderness excursion is the float plane trip over the beautiful Misty Fjords, with stunning views of alpine lakes and steep-sided channels that were carved by retreating glaciers.

Juneau is named after one of the prospectors who discovered gold here in 1880 and this scenic state capital contains local sights ranging from the Red Dog Saloon to the Governor's Mansion. Juneau also offers visitors the opportunity to take a float plane or helicopter flight over the sprawling Juneau Icefield. The helicopters land on a glacier so that passengers, wearing special boots, can walk across its icy surface and peer down its deep crevasses. Also popular is the flight to nearby Taku Harbour for a salmon bake at a rustic lodge.

The boomtown of **Skagway** sprang into being in 1897 during the

Klondike Gold Rush and its streets are lined with original false-fronted buildings that now house gift shops and visitor centres. A sleepy village during the winter months, Skagway bustles with visitors throughout the summer. The town is set at the head of beautiful Lynn Canal, bounded by snowcapped mountains, and arriving cruise passengers can ride the narrow gauge railway that retraces the route taken by thousands of gold prospectors as they climbed over the mountains to reach the Klondike.

The fishing port of **Sitka** is the former capital of Russian America and its attractions include St. Michael's Cathedral and the cannon-ringed Castle Hill, where the offical transfer of Alaska to the United States took place in 1867.

The Glacier Route

Ships proceeding beyond the Inside Passage into the Gulf of Alaska will often pull into Yakutat Bay, where the massive Hubbard Glacier presides over this mountain-ringed bay. Prince William Sound, situated at the top of the Gulf of Alaska, contains Alaska's highest concentration of tidewater glaciers and is the highlight of a glacier cruise. Its mainland shores are surrounded by snowy peaks and indented by dozens of glacier-carved fjords.

A northbound glacier cruise usually terminates in the fishing port of **Seward,** on the Kenai Peninsula, where passengers board coaches for a scenic, three-hour drive to Anchorage where they connect with land tours or a flight home. A city surrounded by wilderness, **Anchorage** is an interesting blend of modern metropolis and Alaskan bush town. On clear days, Mt McKinley – North America's highest peak – can be seen from downtown Anchorage.

The Atlantic islands

The **Azores**, resort islands of beaches and vineyards, were reached by Portugese sailors in the early 1400s and were once the site of naval battles between England and Spain. Today this far-flung outpost of

Portugal is the site of NATO air bases. Ponta Delgada is a popular port of call.

The verdant, mountainous **Madeira Islands**, lying 350 miles off Morocco, were known to the Romans as the Purple Islands. Rediscovered by the Portuguese in the early 1400's, settlement took place under the orders of Prince Henry the Navigator. The British temporarily occupied the islands in the early 19th century but they are today an autonomous region of Portugal. Their steep slopes are covered with patchwork fields of green and dotted with villages of red-roofed white houses. Flowers such as bougainvillaea and hibiscus flourish here and the one of the world's highest sea cliffs – Cabo Girao – provides a spectacular ocean view. The port of **Funchal** was a favourite winter retreat of Sir Winston Churchill who came here on painting holidays. Situated on a beautiful harbour at the base of a mountain, Funchal has a bustling local market where fresh flowers, hand-sewn linens and wickerwork are sold. Fine local wines can be enjoyed at one of the bodegas and afternoon tea is served at the classic Reid's Hotel.

Spain's **Canary Islands**, volcanic in origin, have a recorded history dating back to 40 BC. An important base for voyages to the Americas, they were frequently raided by pirates and privateers such as Sir Francis Drake who was fended off in 1595. The islands visited by cruise ships are **Gran Canaria, Tenerife** and **Lanzarote** with its black and red beaches, bubbling geysers and grottoes containing emerald-coloured water. Las Palmas, only 67 miles from the African coast, is the capital of **Gran Canaria**. Cruise passengers can visit the house in which Columbus once stayed or head to the sand dunes and beaches at nearby Maspalomas.

At **Tenerife** the ships dock in Santa Cruz where duty free shops await visitors. To the south are resorts and beaches of soft volcanic sand. The snowcovered summit of Mt Teide – the highest point in Spain – dominates the island, its valleys filled with banana and pineapple plantations.

Morocco is often included in cruises to the Atlantic Isles and one of its popular ports is **Casablanca,** well known to fans of the classic Hollywood film of the same name. Casablanca was also where the Allied leaders met in 1943. From there visitors can embark on excursions to Marrakech, an ancient red-walled Royal City of narrow alleyways, sultan's gardens, palaces and an atmosphere evocative of the Arabian nights. **Tangier** is another fascinating Moroccon port situated at the crossroads of Europe and Africa. Visitors can stroll the winding, hilly streets, each one featuring a different group of artisans where you can bargain for handcrafted goods. Other attractions are a Sultan's garden and the palace of Dar el Makhzen. Nearby Kasbah, features a palace protected by fortress walls

Bermuda

The number of cruise ships allowed to visit Bermuda is closely monitored to prevent this island group from become overcrowded. Cunard's *QE2* calls a few times each year at Bermuda while a handful of other cruise lines offer regular sailings out of New York from May until October. With 55,000 people living in an area of of 21 square miles, Bermudans have also taken measures to prevent traffic congestion and air pollution by allowing only one car per family. Visitors can tour the interconnecting chain of islands on rented mopeds, in hired taxis or on the local blue-and-pink buses.

There are three cruise ship ports in Bermuda – King's Wharf at West End, Hamilton Harbour and St George – and most ships visit two of them although some will remain at one port. Distances between ports are not great and, during a typical four-day stay, it's easy to see the entire island chain regardless of where your ship docks and becomes a floating hotel. Many people head to the south coast where beautiful beaches range from long stretches of pink sand to tiny, protected coves. Diving and snorkelling are excellent in the clear waters of these reef-ringed islands. Only two miles across at its widest point, Bermuda has over a hundred beaches and eight golf courses. Other natural attractions include caves, grottoes and sea arches.

Bermuda is a British dependency and was discovered by Virginia-bound

British colonists in 1609 when they were shipwrecked on these islands. Their maritime and colonial history can be seen when strolling in King's Square in St George or visiting Gibb's Hill Lighthouse and the local museums. Avid shoppers enjoy Hamilton, commercial centre of Bermuda, where shop-lined Front St overlooks the harbour.

The Caribbean

Cruise ships began visiting the Caribbean in the 1960s, when jet planes became the new mode of transatlantic travel and shipping companies sought new roles for their gracious ocean liners. Today the Caribbean is the most popular cruising area in the world, and for good reason. The allure of this island-dotted turquoise sea is legendary, but natural beauty is not its only attribute. Each of the Caribbean's diverse island nations has its own history and eco-system, which have shaped its inhabitants and their societies.

The British, French, Dutch and Danish all explored these islands in the wake of Spanish expeditions first led by Christopher Columbus. Spain initially established forts along the Caribbean mainland and on most of the Greater Antilles – the larger islands of the West Indies. Other European nations scooped up the smaller islands – the Lesser Antilles – left unclaimed by Spain. Meanwhile the native inhabitants were all but obliterated by European colonialism; only a pocket of surviving Carib natives now survives on Dominica. Africans were brought to these islands as slaves to work on the sugar plantations and they are today the dominant racial group of the Caribbean, setting the tone with rhythmic music and bold colours.

Some of the islands are volcanic in origin, with mountainous terrains, while others are low coral islands. Most are ringed with beautiful beaches bordered by palms and tropical flowers. Caribbean in origin, and often seen slung between two palm trees, is the hammock – which aptly sums up the relaxed pace and mood of these sun-blessed islands.

From the cruising point of view, the region is divided into the eastern, western and southern Caribbean, each forming a distinct itinerary with its own ports of call (see the map opposite). Ships operate from a variety of 'base ports', mostly in Florida.

Base ports

San Juan on the island of Puerto Rico was founded in 1508 by Ponce de Leon. A major Spanish port, it contains El Morro – the most extensive fortress in the Caribbean. Today this city of narrow cobbled streets and sunny plazas is the capital of Puerto Rico and a base port for cruises of the Eastern and Southern Caribbean. A local museum is devoted to Pablo Casals, the Spanish virtuoso cellist who settled here.

Other base ports for the Caribbean are located in Florida and include **Fort Lauderdale**, a popular retirement community and tourist destination with its six miles of soft sand beaches and canal-lined residential streets with yachts moored in front. **Miami** is another major port, especially for cruises to the **Bahamas** where turquoise-green water, white beaches, the British colonial architecture of Nassau and the beach resorts on Paradise Island draw plenty of visitors. **Tampa** and **Port Canaveral** (with its proximity to the Kennedy Space Centre and Disney World) are also used by cruise ships.

Western Caribbean ports

At **Cancun**, located on the Mexican mainland, a modern international resort has been built and shore excursions can be taken to view pyramid-shaped temples at the ancient Mayan city of Chichen Itza. **Cozumel** is Mexico's only Caribbean island and the snorkelling here is superb in the extremely clear waters. Mayan ruins can be visited at the walled city of Tulum on excursions to the mainland.

The British island of **Grand Cayman** also has clear waters for diving and visitors can take submarine rides over the island's extensive coral reefs. Georgetown is the port of call and an international banking centre. Seven Mile Beach is another attraction of Grand Cayman.

Ships visiting **Jamaica** often call at Ocho Rios, where a popular excursion is walking up the tiered bed of the spectacular Dunn's River Falls.

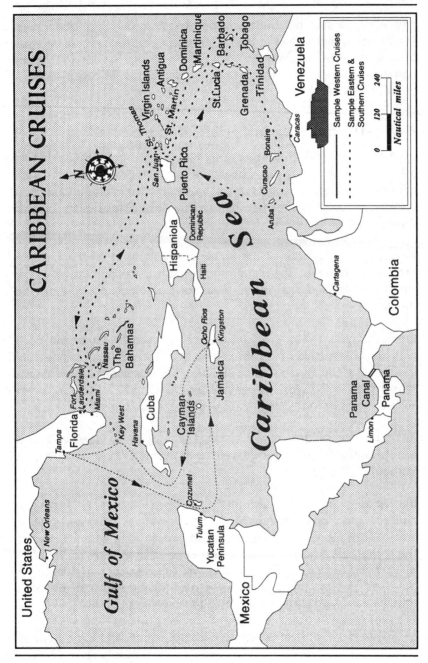

CARIBBEAN CRUISES

Key West, Florida, is included in some Western Caribbean itineraries. The most southern point of the US mainland, Key West is only 60 miles from Cuba. This pretty town of tree-lined streets has long attracted bohemians and artists. Ernest Hemingway's former residence is now a popular museum.

Eastern and southern Caribbean ports

Aruba, Bonaire and Curacao are the ABC of the Dutch Antilles that lie off the coast of Venezuela. **Aruba**'s port of call is Oranjestad, its Dutch heritage captured in gabled terrace houses painted in bright Caribbean colours. Aruba offers fine beaches and clear water for snorkelling and diving.

Bonaire's tiny harbour of Kralendijk is a pretty port with a bustling market place. Again, the island offers good snorkelling with its pastel corals and tropical fish. Huge flocks of pink flamingos live on the island.

Curacao's Willemstad is quite possibly the prettiest Caribbean port, with its golden-coloured gabled houses. Other historic architecture includes the Old Dutch Church (built in 1769) and one of the oldest synagogues in the Western Hemisphere, built in 1732. Curacao is well known for its orange-flavoured liqueur of the same name.

Antigua, one of the Leeward Islands, has beautiful beaches and a British colonial history, evidenced by Nelson's Dockyard at English Harbour.

Barbados is the most British of the Caribbean islands. Cricket is the national sport and the capital of Bridgetown has its own Trafalgar Square with Nelson's Column. The standard of living here is high and the scenery diverse. The island's west coast is lined with lovely swimming beaches; the rugged east coast, exposed to the Atlantic, is pounded by surf; and the interior is criss-crossed with narrow roads that lead through villages and past sugarcane plantations.

La Guaira is the port of access to **Caracas**, capital and largest city of

Venezuela. Founded by the Spanish in 1567, the city is bordered by mountains to the north and hills to the south and, being more than 3000 feet above sea level, has an ideal climate. Almost completely destroyed by an earthquake in 1812, Caracas is a modern city which experienced heavy immigration from Europe following World War II.

Cartagena, Columbia, was founded in 1533, its massive walls built to defend the port against marauding pirates. The view from its 17th-century monastery is of Iberian style palaces, shady plazas and narrow cobblestone streets, where boutiques are housed in medieval dungeons.

Dominica, one of the least developed of the Caribbean islands, was named by Columbus who sailed by on a Sunday. The island's lush and mountainous terrain consists of untouched rainforest, hundreds of rivers and streams, and numerous waterfalls. Dominica offers some of the best wilderness hiking in the Caribbean.

On **Grenada**, the Spice Island, warm breezes carry the fragrance of cinnamon, nutmeg, cloves and vanilla. The capital of St George consists of a circular inner lagoon lined with pastel-painted warehouses and gabled buildings.

The tiny and unspoiled **Grenadines** contain private islands of pristine beaches and clear waters for snorkelling.

Guadeloupe consists of two distinctly different islands – one is mountainous and volcanic in origin and the other is a flat, coral-formed island ringed with white beaches. A French stronghold since 1635, its Creole culture mixes French, African and Indian influences.

Martinique was the birthplace of Napoleon's Josephine. Visited by Columbus in 1502, the island was colonised by the French in 1635. A mountainous island, its valleys are lush with sugar cane and pineapple plantations.

St Kitts was first colonised by the British in 1623 and the main port of Basseterre contains Government House and the Old Court House. It takes four hours for a leisurely drive around this entire island, with stops along the way such as Brimstone Hill Fort, affording views across the water to its Dutch sister island of **St Eustatius**.

St Lucia, fought over by the British and French, is a lush and mountainous island containing one of the Caribbean's most famous landmarks – the Pitons, which are twin conical peaks overlooking Soufriere Bay. Another beautiful spot on St Lucia is Marigot Bay, which was used as a setting for the film *Dr Doolittle*.

The Dutch and the French decided to share the island of **St Maarten/St Martin**. Philipsburg is the Dutch port where good shopping bargains can be found. It's a short drive across island to the French side and the pretty port of Marigot. Fine beaches, golf links, and sailing on board an America's Cup 12-metre yacht are some of the attractions for visitors to this popular island.

St Thomas is the busiest island for ships cruising the Caribbean and its capital, Charlotte Amalie, has extensive dock facilities to accommodate the thousands of passengers who disembark here. A free port, Charlotte Amalie was founded by the Danes in the late 17th century and was the centre of Danish colonial life. Today it's the administrative centre of the US Virgin Islands and its many shops tempt visitors with bargains in jewellery and other duty-free items. Beautiful beaches abound on St Thomas and the neighbouring island of **St John**.

On the undeveloped island of **Tobago**, visitors can enjoy sunbathing, snorkelling, swimming at Pigeon Point or a glass-bottomed boat ride to Buccoo Reef.

Tortola, the largest of the British Virgin Islands, is an island of shimmering white sand and uninhabited satellite islands where a day can be spent on a secluded beach.

The Far East and South-east Asia

Hong Kong – a free port and bustling trade centre – is the hub of banking and shopping in the Far East. Currently a British colony, it occupies Hong Kong Island, Kowloon peninsula, and a mainland area adjoining Kowloon that, along with two bays and 235 offshore islands, was leased from China for 99 years in 1898. Hong Kong's waterfront, its famous skyline a jungle of gleaming skyscapers, bustles with marine traffic which includes traditional junks for ferrying visitors around the harbour. On shore the narrow streets are lined with food stalls, fortune tellers and bazaars. World famous for its shopping, Hong Kong is widely known as the place to buy designer clothes and luxury goods. A funicular whisks visitors to the top of the Peak for a sweeping view of the area.

Comprised of four main islands and many smaller ones, **Japan** is mainly mountainous, with forested slopes, rushing rivers and fertile plains. A number of its peaks are volcanic, the most famous being Mt Fuji, which last erupted in 1707. This perfectly formed, snowcapped cone is sacred to the Japanese and a popular subject for artists. Ports of call include **Kagoshima** on the island of Kyushu, where passengers can visit Samurai houses and formal Japanese gardens, and **Kobe** – the gateway to western Japan. Nearby at Nara and Kyoto (former capital of Japan) are temples, shrines, gardens and shoguns' palaces. The shogun and samurai classes of feudal Japan were abolished in the late 1800s and Japan is today a modern industrial state and constitutional monarchy. Its unique history lives on, however, in the Shinto temples, bonsai gardens and traditional kabuki plays.

The volcanic islands of **Indonesia**, which number in the thousands, stretch along the equator from New Guinea to the Malaysian mainland. Called the Dutch East Indies when merchant ships from the Netherlands dominated local waters during the spice trade, Indonesia gained independence following World War II. The islands' fertile soil supports 70% of the population in agriculture. **Bali**, 'Morning of the World', is one of Indonesia's most beautiful islands. Its verdant hills are covered with terraced rice fields and the island contains numerous Hindu temples, banyan groves and beaches. The Balinese people are noted for their physical beauty, their gentle and artistic natures, and their uniquely ritualistic forms of music, folk drama and dance. No trip to Indonesia is complete without a visit to Bali.

Malaysian ports of call include **Kota Kinabalu** at the base of Mt Kinabalu. Nearby at Mengkabone is a village built on stilts over the water. **Penang** is one of nine states that make up Malaysia. Its capital of Georgetown contains street stalls, trishaws for hire and gilded temples, not to mention the venerable Eastern & Oriental Hotel and other British colonial architecture.

Highly regulated **Singapore,** located off the southern tip of the Malay Peninsula, is renowned for being clean and crime-free. Purchased by the British East India Company in 1819 through the efforts of Sir Thomas Raffles, this island, now a republic and the commercial centre of South-east Asia, is an eclectic mix of Arabian bazaars, Hindu and Buddhist temples, and Victorian government buildings. Its five-star hotels, modern office towers and luxurious shopping malls are in contrast to such historical attractions as the Long Bar at the Raffles Hotel or the painstaking restoration of Chinatown.

The Kingdom of **Thailand**, formerly called Siam, retained its independence during European colonisation of the 19th century. Laem Chabang is the port for the capital of **Bangkok**, with its walled Grand Palace – a massive complex of gilded temples and shrines. Thai silk is a popular shopping item and one of Thailand's most memorable images is that of graceful Thai dancers in their bejewelled costumes and ornate headdresses. Other attractions are **Phuket**, the 'Pearl of Siam', the elegant resorts at Pansea beach, and the country's tidy villages, each one dominated by a temple.

Hawaii, the South Pacific and Australia

The exotic islands that lie scattered across the Pacific Ocean have long attracted wanderlust voyagers and today's cruise travellers can retrace the routes of seafaring explorers, most notably Captain James Cook, the first European to chart these remote waters.

Hawaii

The lush and volcanic **Hawaiian Islands** consist of deep canyons, fern grottos and sun-baked beaches of white, golden and black sand. Oahu's hub of **Honolulu** is famous for hotel-lined Waikiki Beach and such out-of-town attractions as Pearl Harbor and the unspoiled valleys of Waimea Falls Park. The former whaling town of Lahaina on the island of Maui is a port that provides access to some of the islands' best beaches and golf courses.

The South Pacific

A member of the Commonwealth, **Fiji** consists of more than 800 islands, only 100 or so of them inhabited. In addition to the islands' beautiful white beaches and turquoise lagoons, ceremonial displays include the changing of the guard at Government House and the native custom of fire walking.

Perched on the edge of the Marianas Trench (the world's deepest ocean trench), the mountainous **Mariana Islands** are covered with thick jungle. They include the former Spanish possession of Guam, which is now American and was a key strategic base during the Vietnam War.

The twin islands of **New Zealand** contain extraordinarily diverse scenery – jagged peaks, fjord-like sounds, rolling hills and sheep-grazing plains, not to mention Rotorua's surreal landcape of volcanic thermal activity which includes spurting geysers and bubbling pools of mud. **Auckland**, located on the North Island, is New Zealand's largest city. Situated on a hilly peninsula and built around 60 extinct volcanoes, it is cosmopolitan in atmosphere, with pierside bars and restaurants overlooking the yacht-filled harbour.

The South Island's city of **Christchurch** (reached from the port of Lyttelton) is situated on the River Avon and is British in flavour, with stately buildings, a Victorian Gothic cathedral, cottage gardens and antique shops.

The volcanic islands of **Samoa** attracted Somerset Maugham, who used Pago Pago as the setting for 'Rain', and Robert Louis Stevenson, author of *Treasure Island*, who spent the final years of his life here and was buried on Mt Vaea 'under the wide and starry sky.'

Remote and beautiful, the **Solomon Islands** have golden beaches and fronded palm trees. They were also the site of fierce fighting during WWII when American and Japanese troops clashed on Guadalcanal.

Australia

The only continent occupied by a single nation, Australia was claimed by Captain Cook in 1770. A few years later, the country's first British settlement – a penal colony – was established on the east coast near where Sydney now stands. Today most of Australia's major cities are located along this coastline of beautiful beaches. Lying offshore is the Great Barrier Reef – largest coral reef in the world. It's comprised of hundreds of individual reefs, islets and coral gardens, and glass-bottom boats take visitors along the reef to view some 400 species of coral and 1500 species of tropical fish.

Brisbane, the capital of Queensland, is a thriving young city of skyscrapers and colonial buildings. **Sydney,** Australia's oldest and largest city, is also the most vibrant, with its world-famous opera house, local beaches that attract surfers and sunbathers, and interesting pubs and restaurants. The southern city of **Melbourne,** Australia's cultural capital, contains three universities, numerous parks and tramcars.

Fremantle, on the southwest coast, has Victorian pubs, hotels and shops, and is the gateway to **Perth,** located six miles inland on the banks of the Swan River. This is wine-growing country as well as the place where Swan Lager is brewed. Cahunu Park is a good place to see kangeroos and koalas – animal species unique to Australia.

The Mediterranean

The Mediterranean is referred to as the 'cradle of civilisation' and its name is derived from a Latin word meaning 'in the midst of lands'. Ancient empires flourished and fell on the shores of this inland sea, leaving behind archaeological sites that fascinate today's travellers.

The sunny Med, bordered by three continents, is divided into four smaller seas: the Tyrrhenian, Adriatic, Ionian and Aegean. The largest rivers flowing into it are the Po, Rhône, Ebro and Nile. The Mediterranean's variety of destinations – each rich in history, art and culture – combined with the region's natural beauty and warm, dry climate – make it the second most popular cruising region in the world.

Egypt

The ancient city of **Alexandria** is the gateway to Egypt and port of access for Cairo. Located at the mouth of the Nile, Alexandria was founded in 332 BC by Alexander the Great and became a great centre of culture. Under his orders the island of Pharos was connected to the mainland by a mole. Ptolemy II oversaw completion of the celebrated lighthouse on Pharos, where it stood as one of the Seven Wonders of the World until destroyed by an earthquake in the 14th century.

Cairo, the capital of Egypt, was founded in 969 AD. A port on the Nile River near the head of its delta, the city includes two islands – one of which is where, according to tradition, the infant Moses was found in the bulrushes. A modern city with wide streets, Cairo is the largest city in the Middle East and Africa, with a population of over 6 million. Its historic quarters contain famed mosques, palaces and city gates, and its many museums include the Egyptian National Museum, a treasury of ancient Egyptian art. Nearby are the Pyramids of Giza, which were built during the Age of Great Pyramids (2680–2565 BC). These three pyramids are the largest and finest of their kind.

Nile cruises are an ideal way to see more of the archaeological wonders of Ancient Egypt. Additional ports of call include **Luxor**, located on the site of ancient Thebes, its great, pillared temple modified by a succession of pharaohs. Across the river, on the west bank of the Nile, lies the Valley of the Kings, where the treasure-filled tomb of Tutankhamun, the Boy King, was discovered in 1926. Those who cruise the Nile, longest river on earth, also have the opportunity to ride on a camel or on board a felucca, the Nile's traditional sailing/rowing vessels.

Sharm-El-Sheikh, a Red Sea port, is rich in biblical history. The

Monastery of St Catherine is dedicated to the memory of the Burning Bush and nearby is Mt Sinai, which Moses climbed to receive the Ten Commandments.

France

The shores of France have much to offer cruise passengers, whether their ship is cruising up the Gironde and Garonne Rivers into Bordeaux wine country or calling at the fashionable ports of Nice, Cannes or Marseille in the south of France. **Marseille**, its harbour lined with out-door cafés and filled with yachts, is France's oldest city, founded by the Greek traders in 600 BC. The island of **Corsica**, bearing both French and Italian influences, has beaches of honey-coloured sand and rolling, forested hills. Its main port of Ajaccio was the birthplace of Napoleon and his former home is open to visitors.

Gibraltar

Here the Pillar of Hercules was said by the Ancient Greeks to mark the end of the world. Visitors to this British colony can ride a cable car to the top of the Rock for a view across the Straits of Gibraltar to Africa. Another attraction is the Barbary Apes, which live here in caves within a nature reserve.

Greece

This is a sunbaked land of mythical gods and goddesses, ancient ruins and lively tavernas. On the island of **Corfu**, visitors will find miles of beaches and a countryside that is lush and green.

The southern half of **Cyprus** has everything you would expect of a Greek island – the tavernas in Limassol, the beach at Paphos where Aphrodite, goddess of love, was born from the spray of the sea, and the imposing castle at Kolossi.

Katakolon is the port for **Olympia**, site of the original Olympic Games when the warring states of Ancient Greece declared a temporary truce every four years.

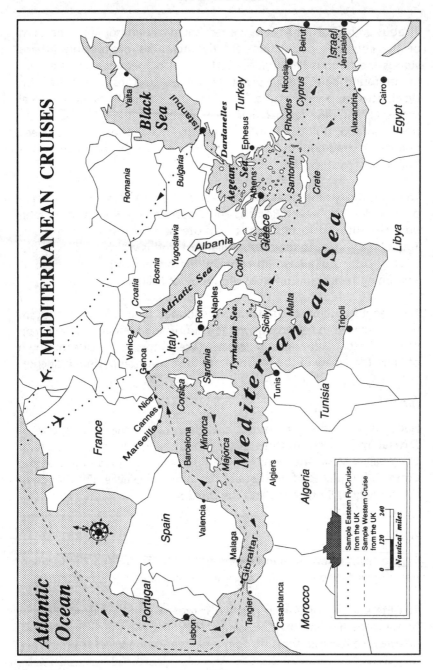

Piraeus is the port of **Athens**, Greece's capital and home to one-third of the country's population. On the Acropolis overlooking Athens stands the famous Parthenon – just one of numerous ancient monuments found here. A funicular takes visitors to a restaurant atop Mt Lycabettus for a view of the Acropolis. Other attractions are the local shops (selling fine leather and silver jewellery), the tavernas where fresh seafood, dolmades and retsina can be enjoyed, and the Greek guards, in traditional uniform, who stand outside the government building.

The walled city of **Rhodes,** on the island of the same name, was occupied by classical Greeks, Romans and Crusaders. The Knights of St John built the massive fortress walls as protection against the Ottomans. Tours take visitors to the nearby village of Lindos which consists of distinctive cubic buildings and contains the oldest temple in Greece. A swimming beach and tavernas are found at Faliraki.

The beautiful island of **Santorini** was formed by a volcanic cataclysm that is believed to have destroyed the flourishing Minoan civilisation on nearby Crete. Cable cars and donkeys take visitors to the cliff-top town of Thira for a view of the harbour and their cruise ship lying at anchor.

Israel

Haifa is the port for visiting the Holy Land. The walled city of **Jerusalem** is sacred to three of the world's religions and is the site of the Wailing Wall, the Dome of the Rock and the 14 Stations of the Cross. Other places of interest are the towns of Galilee, the Church of the Nativity in Bethlehem, and the Dead Sea.

Italy

Centre of the Holy Roman Empire and birthplace of the Renaissance, Italy is a vibrant country of vineyards, palaces and artistic masterpieces.

The Eternal City of **Rome**, reached from the port of Civitavecchia, is home to the Forum, the Colosseum, St Peter's and the Sistine Chapel. **Genoa** also has museums holding great works of art and from the historic port of **Livorno** it is a short excursion into the Tuscan hills to reach **Florence**, where the Medici Chapel and Uffizi Gallery contain famous works by Michelangelo and other Florentine masters.

Romantic **Naples** is situated on the edge of a bay, its surrounding hillsides covered with pastel buildings and the cone of Mt Vesuvius rising in the background. Attractions include the opulent Opera House, drives along the Amalfi Coast, excursions to Pompeii and Herculaneum – the ancient cities that lay buried under volcanic ash for nearly 2000 years – and boat trips across the deep blue waters of the Bay of Naples to the neighbouring island of Capri and the port of Sorrento, beautifully situated on a peninsula separating the Bay from the Gulf of Salerno.

On the island of Sicily, its hills cultivated with vineyards and olive orchards, lies the popular port of **Syracuse**, where ancient monuments include a cathedral built around the remains of the pagan temple of Athena and a Roman amphitheatre.

Venice, one of the world's most romantic ports, is built on 118 islets between which run about 150 canals spanned by some 400 bridges, including the famous Bridge of Sighs. Gondola rides are ever-popular with visitors to this city of Renaissance churches and palaces which seem to float on the water.

Portugal

The capital of **Lisbon**, located on the Tagus River, has both a chic shopping district and a historic quarter of winding alleys, full of bars where the traditional fado songs can be heard. The fishing port of **Portimao**, in the heart of the Algarve, is set among small coves and beaches backed by red cliffs.

Spain

A land of Roman ruins, medieval villages and Moorish architecture, southern Spain annually attracts millions of holidaymakers to its sunny beaches and pleasing countryside of vineyards and orange groves.

Barcelona, site of the 1992 Summer Olympics, is located on the Costa Brava and is the capital of Catalonia and a major seaport, containing surrealistic architecture (Gaudi's Sagrada Familia and Parc Guell), ancient Moorish streets that are too narrow for cars, and the Ramblas – a shopping street of florists, stalls and cafés. The medieval port of Cadiz provides access to **Seville**, the capital of Andalusia, still dominated by the buildings of its Moorish past, including the Giralda tower and the romantic gardens of the Alcazar, as well as boasting the world's largest Gothic cathedral.

Malaga the main port on the Costa del Sol, is overlooked by a hilltop castle and is the gateway to **Granada** – the capital of Moorish Spain, situated high in the mountains of the Sierra Nevada and site of the beautiful Alhambra Palace.

On the island of **Majorca**, amid olive and almond groves, is the cosmopolitan port of **Palma** set on a lovely, yacht-filled bay overlooked by a Gothic cathedral. On the west coast is the village of Deya, former home of the poet Robert Graves, and the monastery of Valledemosa, where George Sand lived with Chopin. Lord Nelson had a villa on the neighbouring island of **Minorca**, overlooking the narrow, hedge-lined lanes of Port Mahon.

Tunisia

This Muslim country, with its muezzins calling people to prayer and many bazaars, contains the site of the ancient city of Carthage, located near modern **Tunis**. Founded by Queen Dido, Carthage was the heart of the Carthaginian Empire and rivalled Rome as a centre of power.

Turkey

Kusadasi and Izmir are the ports for **Ephesus**, an ancient Greek city with pillared porticos, statues and fountains. Antony and Cleopatra walked the marble streets of this 2000-year-old city which was once the cultural centre of the eastern Mediterranean.

Istanbul, ancient capital of the Eastern Roman Empire, was called

Constantinople until 1930. This fascinating city straddles the great Bosphorous Strait and is half in Asia, half in Europe – both geographically and culturally. Famous landmarks of this city of mosques include the Topkapi palace, the magnificent church of St Sofia (now a museum) and the seemingly endless array of stalls in the Grand Bazaar.

Mexico and western California

Mexico has margaritas and mariachi bands, fiestas and fireworks. It also has 2000 miles of Pacific coast, often referred to as the Mexican Riviera. This region of rocky headlands, beaches and holiday resorts is of Spanish heritage, evidenced in the port's town squares and mission churches. The narrow streets and open-air markets bustle with shoppers in search of bargains such as silver jewellery, pottery, embroidered cotton garments and other handicrafts. Bartering is part of the shopping experience in Mexico and this includes negotiating with a cab driver before setting off to see the local sights. Spanish is the official language and informality is the norm, with shorts and sandals acceptable street attire while in port. The pace here is relaxed, the sunsets are superb – and the local beers are excellent.

Ports of call include **Cabo San Lucas** at the southern tip of the Baja Peninsula, **Puerto Vallarta** – a quiet fishing port until *The Night of the Iguana* was filmed here in 1963 and Richard Burton, accompanied by Elizabeth Taylor, helped it become a popular tourist destination – and **Acapulco,** one of the world's most famous resorts. Set on a beautiful bay backed by mountains that are lushly covered with palm trees, Acapulco has long been a favourite haunt of wealthy holidaymakers, among them John and Jackie Kennedy who honeymooned here at a private villa. Acapulco was founded by Spanish explorers in the 1500s and its old quarter contains cathedrals and market squares while its new section is where the luxury hotels and designer boutiques are to be found. At La Quebrada cliff divers plunge 130 feet into a narrow inlet of the sea. Deep-sea fishing charter trips are popular in Acapulco, as are its championship golf courses.

Los Angeles and **San Francisco** are the major Californian ports of a

Pacific coast cruise. Los Angeles is home to Disneyland, Universal Studios, Hollywood and Beverly Hills. Some famous landmarks and attractions in San Francisco are the Golden Gate Bridge, Fisherman's Wharf, Nob Hill, Chinatown and the city's cable cars.

The Panama Canal

One of the world's great engineering feats, the Panama Canal took ten years to build at a cost of thousands of lives and was completed in 1914. Its opening marked the end of a centuries-old era in which ships had to round treacherous Cape Horn at the southern tip of South America when sailing between the Pacific and Atlantic Oceans. Vessels making the eight-hour transit through the Canal's six huge locks are raised or lowered 85 feet. Another attraction of passing through the Panama Canal is the crossing of island-dotted Gatun Lake, where passengers can view tropical plants and exotic wildlife.

As long ago as 1524, King Charles V of Spain ordered a survey of the Isthmus of Panama to determine the feasibility of a faster, safer route for sailing ships. However, a successful attempt to build a shortcut wasn't launched until 1904, when American construction of the canal commenced on land leased from the Republic of Panama. Now called the Panama Canal Zone, it extends for five miles on either side of the canal, which must be constantly dredged. The surrounding terrain of low, lush hills is a pleasing sight for cruise passengers; however, the Panamanian jungle was a breeding ground for malaria and yellow fever before the US military cleared miles of brush and drained swamps in the area to elminate swarms of disease-carrying mosquitoes. The canal was managed by the USA until 1979, when it was turned over to Panama under the terms of a treaty. In the year 2000, control of the canal will transfer to Panama for its continued neutral operation.

Popular ports of call near the Panama Canal include **Costa Rica's** Puerto Caldera, where passengers disembark to travel inland to the capital city of San Jose which is set on a plateau 3800 feet above sea level. Costa Rica's volcanic mountains, lush valleys and virgin tropical rainforests support such an abundance of flora and fauna that nearly one quarter of its total land area is preserved within national parks or reserves. One of Latin America's most politically stable nations, Costa Rica has a democratic government, no army, good roads and safe drinking water.

Scandinavia and the Baltic

With beautiful, bold scenery and clean cities set on the edge of the sea, Scandinavia is an appealing cruise destination. Cruise passengers began visiting Norway's fjords before the turn of the century and they are still coming. Conditions here are ideal for summer cruising, with the days lengthening the farther north your ship travels, and the warm ocean currents providing Norway's coastal cities and villages with a relatively warm and humid climate for a northern country. Bordering the island-dotted Baltic Sea are the capitals of Scandinavia as well as Russia's St Petersburg, built in 1703 by Peter the Great.

Denmark

Copenhagen, the capital of Denmark, has been a trading and fishing centre since the 11th century. It's a charming city of harbours, squares and 18th-century palaces, including the Danish Royal Family's residence. The statue of Hans Christian Anderson's Little Mermaid is a famous landmark, located on the waterfront near Langelinie Promenade.

Finland

In Finland, the golf courses are open 24 hours a day at the height of summer, thanks to the all-day light which its closeness to the Arctic Circle brings. The Finnish are famous for their fine craftsmanship and the capital of **Helsinki** is a major shipbuilding port. The national art gallery and the opera house are just two of the cultural attractions to be found here, along with excellent Russian restaurants.

Norway

Ships cruising the coast of Norway will often anchor at the head of a

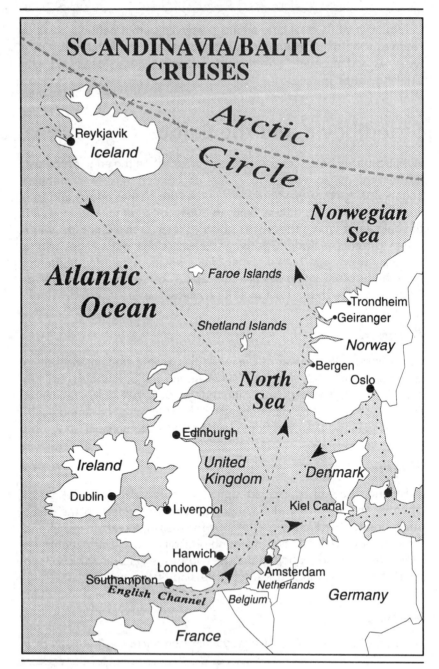

SCANDINAVIA/BALTIC CRUISES

fjord, where passengers can disembark for overland tours through the pristine mountain scenery of lakes, glaciers and waterfalls. Ports of call include **Bergen**, where wooden buildings line old cobbled streets and cable-car rides above the town provide splendid views. The port of **Geiranger** nestles in a green valley at the head of a breathtaking fjord of sheer cliffs, cascading waterfalls and snow-capped mountains.

North Cape is the northernmost point of mainland Europe. Here you can stand at the top of 1000-foot cliffs and see the midnight sun hanging just above the Arctic Ocean.

The modern capital of **Oslo** has impressive public displays of modern art as well as surviving medieval structures. Viking ships that date back to the 9th century are housed in a local museum. **Trondheim**, founded in the l0th century, has a medieval stave church and old timbered houses.

Russia

St Petersburg (formerly Leningrad) was immortalised by the great Russian writers Pushkin, Dostoyevsky and Tolstoy, and was one of the world's cultural centres in the days of pre-revolutionary Russia. Home to the famous Kirov ballet company, St Petersburg also has a university and numerous theatres and museums. Its historic architecture includes the Baroque Winter Palace and the Cathedral of St Peter and St Paul. The famous Hermitage museum, housed in the Winter Palace, was constructed in the neoclassical style and today contains one of the world's foremost collections of art. In June and July, when twilight lingers over St Petersburg, the city enjoys its so-called 'white nights'.

Sweden

The port of **Stockholm**, Sweden's capital, is built on several islands and peninsulas. Founded in the mid-13th century on the site of a fishing village, modern Stockholm is considered one of the world's best planned cities, because of its excellent housing projects, broad streets and numerous parks. The city's historic landmarks include the Church of St Nicholas and the massive Royal Palace.

European river cruises

Much of Europe's history was forged along the banks of its rivers. Empires rose and fell, famous leaders came and went, and all the while the rivers of Europe flowed from their mountain sources out to sea. Over the centuries, the landscapes through which they carved their riverbeds underwent many changes. Hillsides were cultivated, bridges were built and cities were born. To cruise the rivers of Europe is to journey back in time, through the great ages, while enjoying the natural beauty of these timeless waterways.

Shore excursions are usually part of a river cruise package, with prearranged coach tours taking passengers to nearby sights before returning them to the cruise vessel. The rivers plied by these vessels include the **Rhine, Moselle, Main, Danube, Elbe, Rhône** and **Seine**. A guest lecturer is usually on board to explain the local history and entertain passengers with stories about the famous landmarks. When the vessel is underway, passing sights include cliff-top castles, vineyard-covered hills and walled towns. And when the cruise vessel docks at a riverside port, the city sights range from Roman ruins to Baroque monasteries.

Amsterdam is a port of departure when cruising Holland's canals or connecting with a port on the lower Rhine. This city of canals and bicycles is the place to see the world's largest collection of Rembrandt paintings, a museum dedicated to Van Gogh, and Anne Frank's house.

The **Rhine** flows past such historic cities as Strasbourg and Cologne. **Strasbourg**, in the Alsace region of northeast France, was founded in Roman times. Its location at the crossroads of Flanders, Italy and central Europe, made Strasbourg an important commercial centre. Ceded to Germany in 1871 following the Franco-Prussian War, the city was recovered by France in 1919 following World War I. Today Strasbourg is the seat of the European Parliament and remains famous for its beer and goose-liver pâté. **Cologne**'s history also dates back to Roman times, but its famous landmark – the largest Gothic cathedral in Europe – wasn't begun until 1248, its nave and two spires added (according to the original plans) in the late 1800s. The Swiss city of

Basel straddles the upper Rhine and is one of the oldest intellectual centres of Europe: its university was founded in 1460 by Pope Pius II. The city's medieval gates and 16th-century town hall are examples of the local architecture.

The **Moselle** or **Mosel**, a tributary of the Rhine, wends in a southwesterly direction to the German–Luxembourg border, which it traces before reaching its source in the Vosges mountains of northeast France. Its valley slopes are covered with vineyards and dotted with castles. Ports include **Koblenz**, a 2000-year-old city situated at the confluence of the Rhine and Moselle, where Ehrenbreitstein Fortress towers some 400 feet above the river banks. The scenic town of **Cochem** contains cobbled streets and half-timbered houses within the remains of its medieval walls. **Trier**, near the Luxembourg border, is one of the oldest cities in Germany. The main centre of the Moselle wine region, it retains many of its Roman monuments including a fortified gate, an amphitheatre and the basilica. Other historic attractions are its Gothic church and the house where Karl Marx was born, now a museum.

The **Main** connects the Rhine with the Danube, the Main–Danube canal having been completed in 1992. Points of interest on a cruise of the Main include a sidetrip to the completely preserved medieval town of **Rothenburg-ob-der-Tauber** and other picturesque cities such as **Aschaffenburg**, **Miltenberg** and **Würzburg**, treasure houses of Romanesque, Gothic, Renaissance and Baroque architecture. All of these architectural styles are found in **Bamberg**, often described as Germany's most beautiful city. Its early 13th-century cathedral is considered one of the country's finest medieval buildings and the facades of its Old Town Hall are painted with frescoes.

The beautiful **Danube**, great river of central and south-eastern Europe, rises in the Black Forest and enters Austria at **Passau** – one of the most picturesque towns in Bavaria, with its Baroque palace, houses and fountains. Downstream, in Austria's wine-producing Wachau Valley, are the breathtaking sights of **Melk**'s treasure-filled Baroque abbey standing on a promontory above the town, and the old walled town of **Durnstein** overlooked by the craggy ruins of 12th-century

Cruising offers a world of destinations. **Above** The natural wonders of Alaska are becoming an increasingly popular summer destination. **Below** The Mediterranean's historic coasts, and romantic cities such as Venice, have long been a favourite with UK cruise passengers.

Scandinavia and the Baltic states combine breathtaking fjord scenery with ancient and picturesque ports and capitals. Above Nyhavn, Copenhagen.

The Caribbean region offers not only the colour and scenery of tropical islands but also the unforgettable experience of navigating the Panama Canal. **Opposite, top** *Market in Castries, capital of St Lucia.* **Opposite, bottom** *The Crystal Symphony (Crystal Cruises) at Gatun Locks, Panama.*

Above The Far East is the newest area for cruise exploration, taking in exotic sights such as the temples of Wat Suthat, Bangkok.
Below The Nile, pictured here at Aswan, offers the opportunity to see the marvels of Ancient Egypt and the timeless scenery of the world's longest river.

Kuenringer Castle, where Richard the Lionheart was held prisoner. Austria's capital **Vienna,** city of music and centre of the Hapsburg Empire, is filled with grand palaces and cathedrals, opera houses and cafés. **Budapest,** capital of Hungary, consists of two towns – Buda on the right bank and Pest on the left bank. United in 1873 and today linked by eight bridges, this elegant city of palaces and parks, once a capital of the Austro-Hungarian monarchy, has become deservedly popular with Western visitors since the opening up of central Europe.

An ascent of the **Elbe** begins at the German port of **Hamburg** – the nation's second-largest city and busiest port, located near the mouth of the river where it drains into the North Sea. An elegant, modern city and cultural centre, Hamburg is the birthplace of composers Mendelssohn and Brahms, and its noteworthy architecture includes the Baroque St Michael's Church. The Elbe winds past such fascinating ports as **Wittenberg,** where Martin Luther's house is now a museum, and **Dresden,** once a centre of German opera and famous for its Baroque and Rococo architecture, much of it damaged during WWII. **Prague,** situated on a tributary of the Elbe, is the final destination. Capital of the Czech Republic, this scenic city's old quarter is an archi-tectural treasure and was where Mozart wrote *Don Giovanni.*

A cruise of the **Rhône** is a journey through some of France's finest wine country, including Côte de Beaune, Côte d'Or and Beaujolais. At each bend of the Rhône valley is a pleasing landscape of vineyards and hill-side villages. Ports include **Macon** with its magnificent abbey and the opportunity to take a wine tour, and the bustling city of **Lyon,** one of the gastronomic capitals of France.

A cruise of the **Seine** runs between **Paris** and **Honfleur** on the Normandy coast. Stops along the way include **Giverny** – site of Monet's stone farmhouse and beautiful gardens – and **Rouen,** where Joan of Arc was burned at the stake, Flaubert was born and the famous cathedral that intrigued Monet was built.

5 Choosing a cruise line

In Chapter 2 we described, in general terms, the different types of ships and itineraries available to the cruise customer. In this chapter we profile specific cruise lines currently favoured by British passengers, with a brief description of their ships and itineraries.

This cruise lines directory is by no means exhaustive but it does provide an introductory look at what is on offer. Inevitably it uses a few technical terms, but all of these are explained in the Glossary at the end of the book.

Details of special benefits and features, including offers on fares, which are outlined in this chapter are, of course, subject to change; always obtain the advice of a well-qualified travel agent (see Chapter 8, *Booking your cruise*).

Throughout this chapter we use a rating system based on stars like the rating of hotels with which most travellers are familiar. Use these only as guidelines to the general standard of accommodation, cuisine and service on board, and bear in mind that the standard of accommodation will also depend on your your choice of cabin type, and also that every ship has unique features which are not reflected in this broad rating guide. In this system:

3★ signifies a value-for-money budget standard;

4★ is a mainstream ship;

4★+ offers a rather higher standard in this category;

5★ ships are at the top of the range, offering the highest luxury.

Airtours

The recent entry of Britain's second-largest tour operator in the cruise market is likely to have a dramatic effect on the UK holidaymaker's perception of cruising. Operating two renamed 3★ ships, the *Seawing* (formerly owned by Norwegian Cruise Lines) and the *Carousel* (ex-Royal Caribbean Cruise Lines), the Sun Cruises division of Airtours currently offers three summer (March–October) Mediterranean itineraries, all sailing out of and back to Palma, a city already familiar to millions who have spent a summer holiday in Majorca.

Prices are as low as £399 per person, which will ensure that an entirely new section of the holidaying public will be enticed into trying a cruise for the first time. The cruises are aimed especially at the family market, with special reduced prices and facilities for children.

Options include a 7-night fly/cruise, an extended 14-day fly/cruise or a combination of 7 nights cruising and 7 nights on land in a choice of resorts. One itinerary calls at ports such as Ajaccio, Rome and Barcelona, while others take in Sicily, Malta, the Gulf of Sorrento and Sardinia, and Gibraltar, Lisbon and Tangier. Winter options so far (October–April) have taken in not only the Canaries and Cyprus but even a 27-night line cruise from Majorca to and around the Caribbean.

Carnival Cruise Lines

Miami-based Carnival calls its expanding fleet the 'Fun Ships' and fun is what they deliver on a Caribbean cruise. Their informal party atmosphere attracts a high percentage of first-time cruisers – young and old, singles and families – who want to let loose on a holiday in the sun. Public areas are brashly decorated and the cabins are spacious. Feasting, fun and plenty of activities await passengers who book an affordably priced Carnival cruise.

Carnival's 4★ fleet includes four new megaships which carry about 2000 passengers each. Popular round-trip itineraries include three-and-four-day Bahamas cruises from Miami and Port Canaveral, seven-day Eastern and Western Caribbean cruises from Miami, and seven-day

Southern Caribbean cruises from San Juan. Carnival also offers Western Caribbean cruises out of Tampa and New Orleans, and Mexican Baja cruises out of Los Angeles.

Carnival's new *Destiny* is scheduled for delivery in late 1996 and will be over 100,000 tons, with a capacity of over 3000 passengers.

Celebrity Cruises

Few companies have reinvented themselves so successfully as Chandris Inc. did in 1989 when it started a new division of ships with a new name and image to reflect a move upmarket. With the launch of the 70,000-ton *Century* in December 1995, Celebrity Cruises has four 4★+ ships. A fifth ship, *Galaxy*, weighing in at 72,000 tons, is scheduled for completion in December 1996.

This cruise line, well-known for the big 'X' on its funnels, has quickly gained a solid reputation for well appointed ships and fine cuisine. Other ships of the fleet include the 30,000-ton *Meridian*, built in 1963 but completely rebuilt in 1990, and the 47,000-ton sister ships *Horizon* and *Zenith*, launched in 1990 and 1991 respectively. The itineraries are limited mainly to the Caribbean and Bermuda, with the cooler waters of Alaska added to the *Horizon*'s destinations in 1996, Home ports in the Caribbean are Fort Lauderdale and San Juan, while in Alaska the company offers loop cruises of the Inside Passage from Vancouver and line cruises between Seward and Vancouver.

Costa Cruises

This Italian line originated as a transatlantic passenger service in the late 40s, and then ventured into the cruise market in the 1960s. By the early 1980s it had expanded into a worldwide operation. Costa's Italian flair and festive atmosphere have made it popular with British passengers cruising the Mediterranean. Dover is the UK port used by Costa on some of its round-trip and line voyages. The ships in Costa's fleet are elegant, with contemporary styling. The officers are Italian and the service staff is Italian/international. Cuisine is predominantly Northern Italian.

The *Costa Romantica* and *Costa Classica*, 4★+ sister ships, carry 1350 passengers each and 650 crew. Their moderate-sized cabins all come with private bathroom and shower. The smaller sister ships – *Costa Allegra* and *Costa Marina* – each carry about 800 passengers and 400 crew. They are 4★ ships and their relaxed and exuberant atmosphere appeals to young adults. All cabins – almost half of which are inside – contain two lower beds (some of which convert to double beds) and private facilities. A number of Costa ships are ideal for families, with their numerous three- and four-berth cabins as well as such facilities such as a playroom, supervised youth activity centre and babysitting services. Costa itineraries include both fly/cruises and ex-UK to the Caribbean, the Mediterranean and Scandinavia and the Baltic.

Crystal Cruises

With only two 50,000-ton ships, this 5★ cruise line still manages to stop at over 150 ports around the world each year. This is what money will get you – great service, gourmet cuisine, lots of space and a range of itineraries wide enough to excite any globetrotter. The most exotic and remote locations in the world are possible with Crystal Cruises.

The company started out offering both outside and inside cabins with the launch of the *Crystal Harmony* in 1990, but gave up the idea in 1995 with the *Crystal Symphony*, which offers only outside cabins. These are fairly large ships with only 960 passengers on board, so there is a distinct sense of space. The quality of the material throughout the ships is first-class.

CTC Cruise Lines

This British cruise company began operating in 1966 with line voyages to Australia. Today it ranks in the top five in the UK in terms of passengers carried and is the third most popular line for cruises that depart from UK ports on summer cruises to the Baltic, Norway, Canary Islands and the Mediterranean. The atmosphere on board CTC ships is British and informal. The captain, officers and crew are Ukrainian, British and European. The on-board currency is pounds sterling.

The CTC ship most used by UK holidaymakers is the *Southern Cross*, its new flagship. This Italian-built liner, with a distinctive red hull, carries 750 passengers and provides facilities for children (from tots to teens). Suites and cabins all have private facilities and twin beds (a few with double beds). Most have a window or porthole. There are also a limited number of three- and-four-berth cabins as well as single cabins.

Special fares and features
Early booking discount. No single supplements (limited number). No charge for one child sailing with parents; reduced fares for subsequent children. Free Clipper Express coach service between city centre and port in Tilbury (London), Liverpool, Bristol, Leith (Edinburgh) and Greenock (Glasgow). Discount on all National Express network coach services feeding into London Victoria, Liverpool, Bristol, Glasgow and Edinburgh which connect with free Clipper Express service. Air options of flying directly between a regional airport and Amsterdam on KLM (at a discount round-trip fare) for embarkation and disembarkation.

Itineraries
Itineraries of the *Southern Cross* on her debut in 1995 included a maiden voyage from Tilbury to Mexico and the Caribbean, departures from Tilbury to the Baltic and St Petersburg, and to Norway and Iceland; a series of summer cruises from the regional ports of Liverpool, Bristol and Greenock to Madeira and the Canaries, Portugal, North Africa and the western Mediterranean. The final cruise of 1995 for the Southern Cross is a long voyage to Australia via the Suez Canal, calling at many ports in the Indian Ocean and the Far East.

Cunard

This prestigious British line began operations in 1840, when Sir Samuel Cunard, a Canadian pioneer of regular transatlantic steam navigation, formed a fleet of four ships to deliver mail between Liverpool, Halifax (Nova Scotia) and Boston. The Cunard 'Queens' became the line's most famous vessels, starting with the *Queen Mary* and followed by the first *Queen Elizabeth* (named after the Queen Mother while she was consort to King George VI). The largest liner ever built, the *Queen Elizabeth* could outrace any warship on her 1940 maiden voyage across the Atlantic to New York. Her departure from a Scottish shipyard, made under strict Allied secrecy, was so hasty that some unsuspecting workmen were still on board when she headed out to sea.

Cunard's current flagship, the superliner *Queen Elizabeth II* (QE2), is arguably the most famous cruise ship in the world. With a service speed of 28.5 knots, she is certainly the fastest. The rest of the Cunard fleet consists of three different lines – luxury (5★), premium (3–4★) and river vessels. Each ship has a different atmosphere, ranging from the ultimate in luxury and personal attention on Royal Viking Sun to relaxed informality on Cunard's premium ships. Cunard cruises are especially popular with British cruisers in the Caribbean and Mediterranean.

Queen Elizabeth II (QE2)

The *QE2* was designed for transatlantic service but doubles as a cruise liner. Built in the UK, she was launched in 1969 and measures 66,451 tons, with 13 passenger decks. The ship carries 1800 passengers and 1000 crew. Passenger breakdown on transatlantic crossings is 41% British, 40% American and 19% other nationalities.

Officers and crew are British; hotel staff are British and international. The currency on board is the US dollar except on European cruises, when it's pounds sterling. Major credit cards accepted. Traveller's cheques can be converted into local currencies.

The *QE2* is extremely spacious with a high level of passenger service. Cuisine and degree of formality varies from dining room to dining room (which are allocated according to grade of cabin, differentiated by the names Grill, First and Transatlantic class – the *QE2* is one of the few remaining cruise ships to have a class system). The rest of the ship is open to all classes of passengers except for the Queen's Grill Lounge, which is exclusively for the use of Grill Class passengers.

The QE2 underwent a complete refit at the end of 1994 (not without some well-publicised problems, now no more than a bad memory). Notable features include a superb library and excellent children's facilities, with supervision provided by English nannies. The interior decor has recently been modified from its original 60s style to a more traditional art deco look that many passengers expect of a legendary superliner.

Special fares and features of the QE2
Scheduled Wedding Anniversary Cruises offer discounts on cabins and complimentary flowers and champagne to couples celebrating a wedding anniversary. Special benefits to first-time cruisers who book a scheduled Newcomers Cruise and purchase an all-inclusive package entitling them to First Class return rail fare to Southampton or car parking in Southampton, a free shore excursion at a selected port of call and all tips for dining room and cabin staff.

Itineraries of the QE2
Transatlantic crossings scheduled from April to December. Scheduled in between her crossings, and from January to April, are cruises of various areas, such as Florida, Bermuda, Scandinavia, the British Isles, New England and Eastern Canada, the Mediterranean, the Canary Islands and the Caribbean. The *QE2* also offers round-the-world cruises.

Cunard Royal Viking

The ships in this 5★ division of Cunard include the *Vistafjord*, *Sagafjord* and *Royal Viking Sun*, which are medium-sized ships carrying 600–700 passengers and 350–400 crew. The Finnish-built *Royal Viking Sun*, recently acquired by Cunard, is one of the highest-rated ships in the world. Extremely luxurious, spacious and ultra-contemporary but with classic appointments such as teak decks and walk-in wardrobes in all staterooms, the ship carries about 750 passengers and 460 crew.

The officers of these ships are Norwegian and service staff are European and Asian. Scandinavian decor, refined elegance and a relaxed ambiance are part of the luxury service passengers expect on board these classic cruise liners. Currency on board is the US dollar. Major credit cards are accepted. Traveller's cheques can be converted into local currencies.

Special fares and features of the Vistafjord and Sagafjord

Special deals have included the following (check with your travel agent for the latest ones): combination cruises, i.e. take two consecutive cruises and enjoy a significant reduction in the cost of the lower-priced cruise. Free off-airport parking at Heathrow and Gatwick, and at port of Harwich or Southampton. Free regional flights to and from London. Free first class British Rail service from local station to London airport or port of embarkation.

Itineraries of the Vistafjord and Sagafjord

Vistafjord 's itineraries include: the South Pacific, South America, the Caribbean, Bermuda, transatlantic, the Mediterranean, the Holy Land, Western Europe, the Baltic, the Canary Islands. *Sagafjord's* Itineraries: world cruise, the Panama Canal, Bermuda, the Caribbean, Alaska, New England/Eastern Canada, transatlantic, the Mediterranean and the Caribbean.

Special fares and features of the Royal Viking Sun

Benefits and offers are the same as those offered to *Sagafjord* and *Vistafjord* passengers, plus chauffeur-driven transfer within the Home Counties to and from the port of Tilbury; also, on designated cruises repeat passengers are entitled to special on-board gifts and events.

Itineraries of the Royal Viking Sun

The Panama Canal, Bermuda, Eastern Canada, Scandinavia, Ireland, Scotland, Western Europe, the Mediterranean, transatlantic, South America, the Caribbean and round-the-world cruises.

Sea Goddess I and II

These highly-rated twin vessels offer yacht-like luxury with an intimate ambiance and personal service (90 crew serving 116 passengers). Suites are all outside and passengers can dine en-suite whenever they choose, 24 hours a day. The dining room and other public areas are elegant and inviting, with a private club atmosphere. Officers are Norwegian, the service staff European. In addition to a swimming pool and gymnasium, a water sports platform on the stern allows passengers to swim, snorkel, sail and ski right off the ship. These intimate ships can manoeuvre into small ports and anchor off uninhabited islands. Their principal itineraries include the Caribbean, Far East and Mediterranean.

Cunard Countess/Cunard Dynasty

The ships in this premium (4★) division of Cunard are designed for the active holidaymaker who is looking for a more casual atmosphere than is found on the luxury line of Cunard cruise ships. These are mid-sized cruise ships with generous amounts of deck space and an easy-going environment.

Although the currency on board both these ships is the US dollar, they cater specifically to the British cruise passenger. Traveller's cheques (best bought in US dollars) can be cashed on board the ships. Major credit cards are accepted. Cabin electrical outlets are dual standard 110/220 volts.

Typical of this division is the *Cunard Countess*. The ship's officers are British and the service staff is international. Stationed year-round in the Caribbean, the *Countess* carries 800 passengers and 360 crew. The ship makes one- and two-week round-trip Caribbean cruises out of San Juan, Puerto Rico. A one-week Caribbean cruise can be combined with a one-week stay at a resort on either St Lucia or Barbados (flying there to rejoin the ship).

The *Dynasty* is more upmarket than the *Countess* but not as luxurious as Cunard's Royal Viking division. It has contemporary styling and decor, including large picture windows in the public areas and plenty of open decks with sunbathing areas. Deluxe rooms contain two beds that convert into a double bed; standard rooms have a bed and upper berth, all with private facilities (shower). The officers are European and the service staff are Filipino. The ship carries 820 passengers, 320 crew.

The *Cunard Dynasty* cruises the Western Caribbean and Mexican Riviera in winter, making 12-to-22-night line voyages between Fort Lauderdale, Acapulco, Los Angeles and Vancouver. Summer cruises are to Alaska, round-trip from Vancouver, and these can be combined with an overland tour to the Canadian Rockies.

Special fares and features of the Cunard Countess
Exclusive flights to the Caribbean from London Gatwick and Manchester. Luggage checked in for the flight is transferred automatically to your cabin on the ship. Free or low-cost regional flights from selected UK airports. Price includes transfers between San Juan airport and ship. Gratuities for dining room and cabin staff included in fare. Special 'SeaSports' programme that combines an on-board fitness regime with optional activities ashore, including pre-arranged tee and court times at top golf courses and tennis courts, as well as lessons in snorkelling, scuba diving and windsailing.

Special fares and features of the Crown Dynasty
The *Cunard Dynasty*'s offers include Cunard charter or scheduled economy class flights between UK, Fort Lauderdale, Miami, Acapulco, Los Angeles and Vancouver. (Luggage is transferred directly to your cabin, as with the *Countess*.) Free or low-cost regional flights from selected UK airports. Fare includes overnight accommodation (room only) in Acapulco and Vancouver (if part of itinerary), and transfers between airport and ship in cities of embarkation and disembarkation. Gratuities for dining room and cabin staff included in fare.

Cunard Luxury River Cruises

Cunard's five-vessel fleet, operated in association with Peter Deilmann Cruises, offers cruises of the Rhine, Rhône, Danube and Elbe. The majority of these cruises are seven days in length, with additional 10- and 11-day cruises available on the *Prussian Princess*.

These 4- and 5-star vessels resemble floating hotels. On board are an elegant dining room, boutique, beauty salon, library, intimate lounges and bars. Staterooms are finely appointed, each with a private bathroom containing a shower.

Fred Olsen Cruises

Founded in the mid-sixties, this cruise company began with the sharing of vessels by two well-known Norwegian shippers – the Fred Olsen Line and the Bergen Line. In summer their vessels served as passenger ferries on North Sea routes between Newcastle upon Tyne and Norway; in winter they cruised from London to Madeira and the Canary Islands.

The popular *Black Prince* was eventually converted in 1986 to a full-time cruise ship and, in addition to autumn and winter cruises to the Mediterranean and Canary Islands, now sails to the Baltic each summer. UK passengers looking for a good-quality cruise at a budget price often book onto the *Black Prince*, which offers convenient departures from British ports. The ship was built in West Germany in 1966. At 11,209 tons and 465 feet in length, she carries 446 passengers and 200 crew. Officers are European and the service staff is Filipino and Thai. It's a well-maintained, comfortable and friendly ship that attracts a large number of repeat passengers.

Delta Queen Steamboat Company

This division of Fred Olsen offers cruises on authentic stern-wheel paddlesteamers on several American rivers, including the Mississippi, Cleveland, Tennessee, Ohio and Arkansas rivers.

Holland America Line

In business since 1873, HAL operated a successful service from Rotterdam to New York for decades before turning to cruises in the early 1970s. Holland America's Dutch officers and service staff of Indonesians and Filipinos have built a solid reputation of efficiently-run ships, with a high standard of friendly service.

Dark blue hulls and teak decks are standard features of HAL ships, their interiors decorated with extensive artwork which includes Dutch paintings and antiques. Fresh flowers grace both public areas and private cabins, adding to the refined atmosphere, which attracts a mature clientele. Cuisine on HAL ships is continental and consistently good.

The HAL fleet consists of eight 4★+ vessels, including four new sister ships built in the 1990s. The four new ships of the *Statendam* class, named after the first of them, launched in 1993, are each 55,000 tons and carry only 1266 passengers. The *Maasdam* and *Ryndam* were launched in 1994 and 1995, and the *Veendam* is to be launched in 1996. These ships have a high space/passenger ratio, thus providing extremely spacious public areas. Their standard cabins are comfortable, all with two lower beds (which can be converted to a double), sitting area and bathroom with shower. Higher-grade cabins have baths and balconies.

The rest of the fleet consists of the company's flagship the *Rotterdam* (a classic ocean liner launched in 1959), the sister ships *Noordam* and *Nieuwdam* (built in the early 1980s) and the *Westerdam* (launched in 1986; stretched in 1990).

Each of the HAL ships has over £1 million worth of art on display, which,combined with the understated decor, generates a feeling of relaxed continental elegance. The new ships have a sliding roof over the main pool – quite handy on cool or wet days in Alaska, for instance – and this area of the ship has a feeling of space which adds extra appeal to the lido parties held on board.

Itineraries
Most of the HAL fleet cruises the Caribbean in winter, using Fort Lauderdale, Tampa and New Orleans as its base ports. In summer, most of the fleet moves to Alaska, where Vancouver is its home port. One ship remains in the Caribbean throughout the summer (in autumn it cruises the eastern seaboard of the United States and Canada) and another provides summer cruises of Europe. Holland America has offered world cruises for a number of years and the *Rotterdam* is often assigned to this marathon voyage. Despite being over 35 years old, this ship has an intensely loyal following and Holland America has yet to make a decision about keeping the *Rotterdam* beyond the launch of a new ship, as yet unnamed, in 1997.

KD River Cruises of Europe

Since 1826, this German-founded cruise company has plied the rivers of Europe. Queen Victoria was one of many heads of state who cruised aboard a KD vessel and elegant service is still a hallmark of these river cruises. Custom-built for river cruising, KD's vessels are fully air-conditioned, with a bar, restaurant, reading room and gift shop. The observation lounge has panoramic windows and there is an outer verandah and sundeck. Most vessels also have a swimming pool, sauna and solarium. Cabins are all outside and they range from deluxe (with two lower beds, minibar and TV) to standard, with upper and lower bed. All cabins have a bathroom with shower.

Special fares and features include wedding anniversary savings; regional airport supplements in Britain; reduced children's fares; Optional Stay packages include accommodation and rail travel.

KD's itineraries include the rivers of Europe – the Rhine, Moselle, Danube, Elbe and Seine – as well as the river Nile. They range in length from seven to 15 days, with optional extended stays at various great cities of Europe or in the Swiss Alps. Regular economy airfare is included in the price of the cruise.

Norwegian Coastal Voyage

The company's name exactly describes its speciality, cruises from Bergen to Kirkenes in the Arctic Circle and back on the coastal steamer *Hurtigruten* and ten other ships. Cabins range from first-class suites to simple double berths, and the ships carry cars for tourists wishing to use the port-to-port service as part of a motoring holiday.

Norwegian Cruise Lines

Currently the fourth-ranked cruise line of choice for British passengers in the Caribbean, NCL pioneered the concept of Caribbean cruising in the late sixties. Originally called Norwegian Caribbean Lines, the company introduced the first Caribbean cruise out of Miami on board a small, amenity-filled cruise ship called the *Sunward*.

Today NCL's 4★ fleet ranges from ultra-modern cruise vessels to the classic ocean liner *Norway* (formerly the *France*). With the exception of the *Norway* (which is semi-formal), the atmosphere on NCL ships is casual, with an emphasis on activities and entertainment. This cruise company specialises in sports theme cruises hosted by celebrity athletes, and the nightly stage shows are lavish, often featuring well-known entertainers. Officers are Norwegian and the service staff is international. The cuisine is a combination of American and Continental. NCL's newest additions to the fleet are the sister ships *Windward* and *Dreamward*, which each carry 1242 passengers each and 483 crew. Their contemporary design incorporates a great deal of terracing and glass to allow maximum viewing of the passing scenery.

Itineraries
NCL's Caribbean itineraries include seven-day round-trip cruises out of San Juan, Fort Lauderdale and Miami. Also offered are three-day Bahamas cruises out of Miami, seven-day New York–Bermuda cruises during the summer, and three- and-four-day California/Mexico cruises out of Los Angeles. The *Norway* cruises all year round in the Caribbean. The *Windward* heads to Alaska each summer to make seven-day round-trip cruises out of Vancouver.

Orient Lines

Founded in 1992 by British entrepreneur Gerry Herrod, this company's corporate philosophy is one of providing cruises to exotic destinations at affordable prices. The emphasis is on offering interesting itineraries, many of them designed as complete cruise-tours with distinguished guest lecturers and local cultural performances so that passengers get the most out of the foreign ports they are visiting.

The ship used by Orient is the *Marco Polo*, built in Germany in 1966 and extensively rebuilt in 1993. The hull has been ice-strengthened for voyages to Antarctica, the top deck has a helicopter landing pad, and

Zodiac landing craft are carried on board for transporting passengers ashore at remote destinations. A medium-sized ship at 20,502 tons and 578 feet in length, the *Marco Polo* also contains all the amenities you would expect of a modern cruise ship, such as a swimming pool, health club, show lounge and an elegant dining room that serves five-course dinners. Orient's various itineraries cover South-east Asia, the Orient, Russia's Far East, Indonesia, Australia, New Zealand, the South Pacific, India and Africa.

Special fares and features
Advance purchase discounts. Low-cost single supplements. Cruise-tour price includes pre- or post-cruise hotel stays at embarkation cities as well as city sightseeing and transfers. Pre- and post-cruise land tours and extended city stays at reasonable prices. Discounts on consecutive cruises with no repetition of ports of call. Special group airfares.

P & O Cruises

This British cruise company began operations in 1837 – the year Queen Victoria ascended the throne. Originally called the Peninsular Steam Navigation Company when running mail to Spain and Portugal ('the Peninsula'), the company expanded its services and became the Peninsular & Oriental, offering service to Bombay and Australia as well as cruises to the fjords of Norway, the Mediterranean and the Caribbean. Among those who embarked on P & O cruises were William Thackeray and America's Mark Twain.

P & O is still Britain's favourite cruise line, both for its affordability and the atmosphere on board its ships which – as stated in its brochures – is utterly British. Whether a passenger simply wants a decent cup of tea or would like to pursue a special interest during the cruise, be it bird-watching or bridge, P & O has maintained its solid reputation among British cruise travellers.

Special fares and features of the P & O fleet
There are a number of P & O special fares and features that apply to the entire fleet. Generous discounts are currently given for children,

with children under 2 years receiving a heavy discount on the adult fare. Passengers sharing a four-berth cabin also receive discounts and reduced group fares are available upon request. Booking two consecutive cruises qualifies passengers for a discount on the combined fare. And passengers who can take a cruise on three weeks notice and are flexible regarding the choice of ship, cabin type and itinerary, may want to register with P & O's Take A Chance scheme for a significant reduction in the fare.

Honeymoon packages are available on any cruise, and anniversary packages are available on specified cruises. A few selected cruises also offer a newcomers' package for first-time P & O passengers. Numerous theme cruises are available, including the following: arts and crafts, birdwatching, bridge, classical music, cricket, gardening, golf, photography, Scottish highland dancing, sequence dancing.

Oriana

Oriana is P & O's newest ship and her maiden voyage was in April 1995. Specifically designed and built for the British cruise market, this superliner is 67,000 tons and 850 feet in length, with 11 passenger decks and a cruising speed of 24 knots.

The *Oriana* has combined state-of-the-art ship design with the company's traditional home-away-from-home ambiance which appeals to British passengers. A one-class ship with all the facilities one would expect on a ship this size – three swimming pools, nine bars and extensive children's facilities – the *Oriana* also has some stunning features to remind her passengers that they are cruising on board one of P & O's legendary liners. The ship's centrepiece is a four-deck atrium with a cascading waterfall and spiral staircase. Nestled at its base is the lush greenery of the Garden Court, opposite the Reception Desk.

All cabins contain private facilities with a shower or bath (depending on the grade of cabin), as well as a refrigerator, television and safe. Two-bedded cabins contain either a double bed or two lower beds. Three-berth cabins contain two lower beds and one upper berth; four-berth cabins have two lower beds and two upper berths. Staterooms have a double bed or two lower beds with separate sitting area. Outside cabins come with picture window or porthole, and premier cabins have a jacuzzi, sitting area and balcony.

The British-registered *Oriana* holds 1760 passengers and 760 crew. The ship's officers are British and service staff are international. The currency on board is pounds sterling and both traveller's cheques and personal cheques (supported by a cheque card) can be cashed. Foreign currency is also available for most countries visited. Major credit cards accepted but not for the purchase of cash.

Special fares and features of the Oriana
Escorted tours of Australia and Japan on applicable segments of *Oriana*'s world cruise. Extended three-night stays at various ports of embarkation or disembarkation, which includes first class hotel, breakfast, transfers between ship, hotel and airport, all local and state taxes, and porterage.

Itineraries
Three-month world cruise, departing Southampton, which includes the Caribbean, the Panama Canal, San Francisco, the South Pacific, Australia, New Zealand, South-east Asia and the Mediterranean. (Options include booking one segment of cruise and joining or disembarking the cruise at various ports.) Caribbean cruises – 23-night round-trip from Southampton; 25-night line voyage from Southampton to San Francisco with return flight to London. 19-to-36-night South Pacific/Far East cruises – ports of embarkation and disembarkation are San Francisco, Sydney, Hong Kong and Singapore. 15-night Indian Ocean cruise; from Hong Kong to Bombay; 20-to-32-night Indian Ocean/Mediterranean cruises; ports of embarkation and disembarkation are Hong Kong, Singapore, Bombay and Southampton. 14- and 17-night Mediterranean cruises, round-trip from Southampton.

Canberra

The *Canberra*, which first entered service in 1961, is a long-time favourite with British cruise passengers. Well maintained, with comfortable accommodation and excellent children's facilities, the

Canberra appeals to the budget-conscious cruise traveller. Its facilities and ambiance attract both the mature holidaymaker and families with young children. British and 'colonial' cuisine is served in the dining rooms. Officers are British; service staff are British and international.

The cabins range from outside suites and staterooms to economical inside cabins, many of these without private facilities. Those with private facilities have either a bath or shower. Cabin types include two bedded, two berth and a high number of single cabins, which makes this ship a good choice for solo cruisers. The currency on board is pounds sterling. Traveller's cheques and personal cheques with a cheque card can be cashed on board. Local currencies for ports are available and major credit cards are accepted.

Special fares and features of the Canberra
Escorted tours of Africa and China on applicable sectors of *Canberra*'s world cruise. Also, extended three-night stays at various ports of embarkation or disembarkation, which includes first-class hotel, breakfast, transfers between ship, hotel and airport, all local and state taxes, and porterage.

Itineraries
Three-month round-trip world cruise, departing Southampton (options include booking one sector of the cruise). Caribbean cruises: 22-night round-trip cruise from Southampton; 23-night line voyage from San Francisco to Southampton. Pacific and the Far East: 18- to 22-night fly/cruises, ports of embarkation and disembarkation being Singapore, Hong Kong, Sydney and San Francisco. Africa and Indian Ocean: 15- to 37-night line voyages from Southampton or fly/cruises from Cape Town, with return flights from Cape Town, Singapore, Hong Kong and Sydney. 16-night Mediterranean cruise, round trip from Southampton. 16-night Atlantic Isles cruise, round trip from Southampton.

Victoria

P & O's third ship, formerly the *Sea Princess*, was recently renamed *Victoria* in honour of a former P & O ship launched in 1887 to celebrate Queen Victoria's Golden Jubilee.

A former ocean liner, and more upmarket than the *Canberra*, the *Victoria* is intimate and elegant, with a decor dominated by fine wood panelling and rich fabrics. Passengers, the majority of whom are British, can enjoy the generous open decks and sunbathing areas, especially in the Caribbean, which is the region that this ship focuses on.

Her officers are British; service staff are British and Goan. The cuisine, catering to the British palate and served in a tiered, European-style dining room, is excellent. The *Victoria* is smaller than the other two P & O liners and carries just 715 passengers and 380 crew.

The cabins are very roomy, with good-sized bathrooms containing either a bath or shower and abundant wardrobe/drawer space. Two-berth cabins contain one upper and one lower berth; two-bedded cabins have one berth that folds away; staterooms have two lower beds and a sitting area. Single-berth cabins are also available.

Itineraries

Caribbean fly/cruises: Flights from London/Manchester to San Juan, Puerto Rico. 11- to 15-night cruises of the southern and western Caribbean. Mediterranean 14-night fly/cruises: Flights between London or Manchester and Malaga, Venice and Aqaba, Jordan.

Princess Cruises

Based in Los Angeles and purchased by P & O in 1974, this North American division doubled its fleet in the summer of 1988 when it acquired Sitmar Cruises, an upmarket Italian line. Today Princess operates nine ships and has been an industry leader in its ongoing introduction of new ships that are large, roomy and innovative in design. UK holidaymakers tend to choose Princess cruises for a particular destination, often when planning a cruise to the Caribbean, the Mediterranean or Alaska. The Princess line of ships is also popular with American and Canadian passengers.

Princess provides a consistently high level of service (one crew member for every two passengers). Cabins are generally large, all with private facilities and twin beds that can usually convert to doubles. In-cabin televisions are a standard feature, as are multi-channel radios offering various music stations, and the BBC World Service is often available. Depending on the ship, officers are British or Italian; the service staff is European or international. The Sitmar influence is evident in the fresh Italian pastas served in the dining room and the pizzerias, where peckish passengers can catch a quick, informal meal.

The currency on board is the US dollar. Traveller's cheques should be in US dollars for cashing at the purser's office. Major credit cards are accepted for settling your shipboard account at the end of the cruise.

The Princess fleet

The sister ships *Crown Princess* and *Regal Princess* are 4★+ megaships carrying 1590 passengers and 700 crew. Their officers are Italian; service staff is international. The ships feature roomy cabins, all with walk-in wardrobes, refrigerators and large bathrooms.

The 4★ *Star Princess* carries 1470 passengers and 600 crew, comprising Italian officers and European service staff. The cabins are spacious and well-appointed, and the ship contains playroom facilities for children.

The 5★ *Royal Princess* entered service in 1984 and was christened by Diana, Princess of Wales at the ship's home port of London. It is a favourite with British customers. Carrying 1200 passengers and 520 crew, the ship's officers are British and the service staff is international. All cabins are outside, with full baths; public areas are spacious and elegant.

The 4★ *Sky Princess*, which carries 1200 passengers, attracts a large number of mature passengers. The ship's crew numbers 550 and consists of British officers and European service staff.

The mid-sized *Island Princess* and *Pacific Princess* (4★ sister ships) are elegant and offer an intimate atmosphere popular with mature passengers. Both ships carry 610 passengers and 350 crew. Officers are British; service staff is international.

Sun Princess is the newest addition to the Princess fleet, entering service in December 1995. The world's largest cruise ship at the time of her launching, this megaship is profiled in Chapter 7, *New ships, new horizons*.

Special fares and features
Princess Pricebreakers – large savings on bookings made at least 60 days in advance; 50% off second person's fare. A 'Headstart' programme offers free regional flights to London from anywhere in the UK and a free overnight hotel stay at Heathrow or Gatwick prior to next day's flight, plus free coach connections between London airport and Southampton or free car parking at Southampton. Caribbean cruises feature a day anchored off a private beach hideaway in the Bahamas or the Grenadines.

Newcomer cruises in the Caribbean and Far East welcome first-time cruisers with a special escort on board, a Newcomers Cocktail Party, a bottle of bubbly in their cabin, one complimentary shore excursion, and an on-board credit in dollars for both partners, to spend as they like. Honeymooners qualify for an automatic upgrade of two cabin categories and receive a bottle of champagne in their cabin. Wedding anniversary celebrants receive a free upgrade of one cabin category, a bottle of bubbly and a special cake on the anniversary day.

Itineraries
Caribbean fly/cruises include: 9–16 nights London to Miami – transfer to Fort Lauderdale for round-trip western, southern and consecutive western/eastern Caribbean cruises; nine nights London to San Juan, Puerto Rico – seven-day round-trip Southern Caribbean cruise; 12 nights London to Miami – transfer to Fort Lauderdale for 10-day round-trip cruise which includes the Panama Canal; 12–17-night line voyages between Fort Lauderdale/San Juan and Acapulco/Los Angeles. You can extend your Caribbean cruise with pre-cruise resort stays of two to seven nights at Walt Disney World in Orlando or at Miami Beach; three or seven nights at Nassau, Bahamas; two nights in San Juan; or three nights in Acapulco.

Mediterranean fly/cruises offer: 12-to-14 nights, Rome to Athens (or vice versa), Barcelona to Venice or Southampton to Rome (or vice versa). There are optional pre-or-post cruise stays of one to three nights in any of the above cities. Optional travel to or from Venice on the Orient Express.

Alaska fly/cruises include: nine-night, round-trip cruises from Vancouver; 9- to 10-night line voyages between Vancouver and Anchorage, Alaska (flights from London to either Vancouver or Seattle); 14-night round-trip cruises from San Francisco. Pre- and post-cruise land tours are available: five- to eight-night rail tours of Alaska; four- to seven-night coach/rail tours to the Canadian Rockies; two-night stays in Vancouver/Victoria or San Francisco.

Other cruise destinations are offered, such as: 13-night cruises round-trip from Southampton to Spain and Morocco; Scandinavia; the Baltic; Northern Europe and Ireland; Iceland, Scotland and Ireland.

Royal Caribbean Cruise Line

This cruise company was formed by a pair of Norwegian ship owners in the early seventies. Headquartered in Oslo but based in Miami, RCCL soon set the standard for Caribbean cruising with its fleet of new, sophisticated ships sporting raked bows, midship pools and the company's trademark Viking Crown lounge, which wraps around the funnel and provides passengers with a panoramic view – the perfect vantage point for watching the ship pull away from a Caribbean port as the evening sun sets the sky afire.

RCCL enjoys a strong British following in the Caribbean, where it's second only to Cunard among UK passengers, and it offers a variety of fly/cruise packages to the Caribbean. RCCL's new ship, *Splendour of the Seas*, will be sailing out of Harwich in 1996.

The upbeat and casual atmosphere on board RCCL ships appeals to young, active travellers who enjoy both sophistication and lively entertainment. Families also enjoy the many supervised programmes for children, the special children's menus and the 'teen' discos.

Currency on board all the ships is the US dollar. Visa, MasterCard and American Express cards are accepted for on-board charges. Power points are for 110 volts AC, US 2 flat pin plug requiring dual-voltage shavers and hairdryers with a suitable adapter.

The RCCL Fleet

Sovereign of the Seas, Majesty of the Seas and *Monarch of the Seas* are 4★+ sister ships which carry 2276 passengers and 825 crew – Norwegian officers, international service staff. These handsome mega-ships have spacious and impressive public areas, such as a five-deck-high centrum lobby and glass lifts. Standard cabins are compact and contain two lower beds and a bathroom with shower.

The 4★ *Song of America* carries 1402 passengers and 525 crew – Norwegian officers, international service staff. The ship has spacious public areas and compact cabins, each with two lower beds that can form a double bed and a bathroom with shower.

The *Sun Viking* is the smallest ship in the fleet, carrying 714 passengers and 320 crew, and it offers a more intimate cruise experience than on the larger megaships. Cabins on this 4★ ship are compact but comfortable, some with one lower bed plus Pullman upper, others with two lower beds or one double bed. All cabins have bathroom with shower.

The *Nordic Empress* cruises year-round to the Bahamas on 3- and 4-night itineraries. Carrying 1600 passengers and 685 crew, this 4★+ ship provides a good party atmosphere in a contemporary setting. The officers are Scandinavian and the service staff is mainly Caribbean.

Legend of the Seas is RCCL's newest megaship, launched in spring 1995. Its ultra-modern features include a seven-deck-high centrum lobby and a glass lift that whisks passengers up to the Viking Crown Lounge. On the ship's uppermost deck, at the stern, is an 18-hole miniature golf course. Truly a floating resort, this ship is profiled in detail in Chapter 7.

The *Splendour of the Seas*, due to go into service in May 1996, will operate out of the UK.

Special fares and features
Early booking programme. Free regional flights from selected UK airports to London; reduced rates at selected hotels and car parking facilities near Gatwick and Heathrow. Regular, scheduled, economy-class transatlantic flights or special business class offers with British Airways Club World. Cruise-only reductions for passengers making their own flight, hotel and transfer arrangements. Special prices for single passengers. Honeymoon Programme – champagne welcome and other special benefits; Royal Occasions Programme (for couples celebrating any special occasion) – welcome- aboard bottle of champagne, formal portrait in an engraved frame and other special benefits.

CruiseCombo programmes for passengers who want to extend their stay in Florida, New York or Canada, or on a Caribbean island, or combine two cruises – attractive hotel/resort prices booked in conjunction with their cruises. Golf Ahoy! programme for passengers seeking golf excursions in Bermuda and throughout the Caribbean.

Eastern and western Caribbean cruises all include a stop at Coco Cay, RCCL's private island destination in the Bahamas.

Itineraries
Caribbean fly/cruise holidays (12- to 16-day holidays) offer: nine-day round-trip cruises from Miami to the eastern and western Caribbean; seven- and nine-day round-trip cruises from San Juan to the Southern Caribbean; 12–13-day line voyages from San Juan to Miami; three- and four-night round-trip from Miami to the Bahamas.

Other cruises include: Alaska fly/cruises out of Vancouver; round-trip Scandinavian cruises out of Harwich; Bermuda fly/cruises out of New York; and Mexico fly/cruises out of Los Angeles. New for 1996 is a Far East cruise programme.

Seabourn Cruise Line

Seabourn operates two ships, *Seabourn Pride* and *Seabourn Spirit*. Each holds no more than 200 passengers, ensuring a high level of individual attention and service. Their size enables them to navigate rivers such as the Thames, Loire, Amazon and New York's East River, as well as coastal waters. Officers are Norwegian, crews international.

Between them these ships cover a wide variety of cruise destinations all year round, among the more unusual being South America, Africa and the Seychelles, Vietnam and Myanmar (Burma). Shore excursions are equally imaginative, including hot-air ballooning over the Loire chateaux and receptions in castles and palaces.

Silversea Cruises

Silversea's two small (16,800-ton) Italian-built vessels, *Silver Cloud* and *Silver Wind*, launched in 1994, maintain a high crew-to-passenger ratio of 2 crew for every three passengers, and the high levels of service this implies, together with the atmosphere of luxury and intimacy on board, command a loyal following.

An unusual feature of Silversea cruises is that the price is totally inclusive – all expenses, including drinks, tips and other items which are normally extras – are taken care of in the cruise price. The ships' dining rooms are formal in atmosphere and run on restaurant lines, with passengers choosing their own table and company each night. Three-quarters of the cabins in the luxury all-suite accommodation have their own verandah.

Itineraries
The wide range includes: 8- to 15-day fly-cruises of the Mediterranean, departing from ports such as Haifa, Athens, Monte Carlo and Barcelona; a transatlantic cruise from Fort Lauderdale, Florida, to Lisbon; the Far East, taking in Singapore, Hong Kong, Bombay and Bangkok among other destinations; Scandinavia and the Baltic (departing from London's Tower Bridge and ending in Copenhagen, and vice versa); the Caribbean; and the American East Coast, from New York north to Montreal, passing New England, or south as far as Nassau, calling en route at historic American cities such as Philadelphia and Savannah.

Swan Hellenic Limited

In 1983 P & O purchased a London travel firm owned and operated by R K Swan, who has been operating Mediterranean cruises since 1954. Highly popular with passengers who like to combine learning with relaxation, Swan Hellenic's cultural cruises of the Mediterranean have retained their well-deserved reputation for providing intellectually stimulating experiences. They offer interesting itineraries and guest lecturers from Cambridge, Oxford and other universities are on board to give entertaining talks on the archaeology, history and culture of the areas being visited.

For years these educational cruises took place on board the *Orpheus*, which Swan Hellenic chartered from the Greek-owned Epirotiki lines. Starting in spring 1996 Swan Hellenic will be using its own cruise ship, the *Minerva*. This completely refurbished vessel (formerly a Russian reconnaissance ship) is Bermuda-registered, with a British captain and officers. The ship's passengers, about 300 per cruise, are treated to the traditional Swan Hellenic experience in a sociable and relaxed atmosphere as the ship glides from one historic port to another.

A Swan Hellenic cruise is an all-inclusive holiday combining entertainment with enlightenment, the fare includes all shore excursions and site fees as well as port taxes and gratuities. Passengers also receive handbooks with maps, historical overviews and information on the ports of call.

European river cruises

The *Rembrandt van Rijn* – a modern, spacious vessel carrying 90 passengers – is used for these cruises along the scenic waterways of Europe. All cabins are outside with twin beds and a private bathroom with shower. The three-decked vessel has a dining room, lounge, bar and partly covered sun deck. Each cruise has a knowledgeable guest lecturer on board. All-inclusive cruise price includes flights, accommodation, a full programme of sightseeing, all tips and (if you are a UK resident) comprehensive travel insurance. Itineraries, which range from 5 to 11 days, include the Rhine, Moselle, Main and Danube.

Spice Island Cruises

These expedition cruises of Indonesia are on small ships carrying from 24 to 150 passengers. The emphasis is on exploration and recreation, such as snorkelling and scuba diving. On-board lecturers share their knowledge of local traditions, folklore and natural history.

Thomas Cook Holidays (Nile Fleet)

When the Englishman Thomas Cook founded his company in 1841 and created one of the world's most successful travel agencies, he was tapping into a growing market. Victorians were avid travellers and, it could be said, they were the world's first true tourists as they ventured, often by ship, to far-flung regions of the globe. Cook's formed an early and lasting relationship with Egypt and dominated tourism there. In 1884, they were even able to organise the transportation of an entire British army expeditionary force of 18,000 men up the Nile to relieve General Gordon and his troops, who were under siege at Khartoum.

Thomas Cook Holidays is still sending expeditions up the Nile but these are now on custom-designed river vessels. The Thomas Cook Nile Fleet includes three vessels – the *Royal Rhapsody, Royal Orchid* and *Royal Serenade*, all of which boast exquisite decor, spacious public rooms and extensive sun decks, both open and shaded. Cabins, which number only 27 and include 6 suites, are all finely appointed with thick carpets, two beds, private bathroom with shower and a large tinted window. On the upper deck is a swimming pool, jacuzzi and sunken bar. The overall ambiance is one of being on board a millionaire's yacht with a Tour Manager as host.

Another vessel used by Cook's Nile cruises is the *Eugenie*, named after the French Empress who opened the Suez Canal in 1869. Built in 1993, this ship's classic design and decor evokes Edwardian elegance with such features as wood panelling and mosaic floors. Modern amenities include a swimming pool and jacuzzi on the upper sundeck. Comfortable cabins, all outside, have radio and music channels, and some have private balconies. A crew of 65 serves the 102 passengers.

Special fares and features
Special car parking rates at Heathrow and Manchester airports; exclusive prices for first-class British Rail Intercity travel or National Express coach travel; reduced fares on UK regional flights; reduced rates at airport hotels.

Arranged extensions; personalised itineraries upon request for group bookings; reduced children's rates; complimentary travel bag included with tickets, luggage tags and other travel pack items.

Fully-escorted Cook's Tours of Egypt vary in length from 6 to 17 days, with the Nile cruise portion ranging from 3 to 10 nights, depending on which tour is booked.

Thomson Cruises

Like Airtours, leading tour operator Thomson has opened up the cruise market to thousands of first-timers by applying its experience as a mass-market holiday company. Low prices, special appeal to families and the possibility of combining a short cruise with a beach resort holiday are the features which they share with Airtours. Their single cruise ship *Sapphire* offers five different summer fly/cruise itineraries of 7 to 8 nights, in the Mediterranean, reaching out as far as the Aegean, Israel and Egypt.

6 Your cruise holiday

The wonderful thing about preparing for a cruise is the lack of effort required. Once you are on board the ship, the captain and crew will handle all travel concerns and your time will be your own to do with as you please. So, to ensure you make the best use of your holiday time, this chapter will address some of the questions you may have about your holiday preparations.

Documentation

Passports and visas

The majority of cruise destinations will require that you have a valid, up-to-date, 10-year British Passport. (As of October 1995, the government withdrew British Visitors Passports and a full British passport is now required for foreign travel.) If you do not have a current passport, you should apply at least one month prior to your departure date to allow enough time to obtain one. If your cruise includes an American port, you will need to complete a visa waiver form that will be included with your cruise ticket. Your travel agent can advise if visas are required for other ports of call included in your cruise.

Travel documents

A few weeks before your departure date (and upon payment in full of your cruise fare), the cruise line will send you all pertinent documentation which usually includes your cruise ticket, airline ticket (if applicable), luggage tags, a customs and immigration form, and information on shore tours and other aspects of the cruise, often in booklet form. All of this documentation should be read carefully and a detailed itinerary left behind with a family member, friend and/or neighbour in case someone back home needs to contact you while you're away. Be sure to include your cabin number, the name of your ship, its phone number and the ocean code for the area you will be cruising (e.g. 874 for Atlantic West, which includes the Caribbean and the Gulf of Mexico).This ship-to-shore information should be given in your travel documents, and will assist anyone trying to place a satellite call through the international telephone operator to your ship in an emergency.

Another precaution you should take before leaving home is to photocopy on a single sheet of paper the identification page of your passport (the one with your photo and passport number on it), your drivers licence and any credit cards you will be carrying in your wallet. Keep one copy of this sheet with you (separate from your passport and wallet) and leave another one at home.

Insurance

With most travel agents, you can take out their recommended holiday insurance policy at the time of booking. A comprehensive policy will cover travel cancellation, delayed departure, medical expenses, personal accident and liability, lost baggage and money, and legal expenses. Premiums are about £20 to £30 per person on a two-week European cruise and £50 to £70 for other parts of the world. Children's premiums are usually less, while adults over 65 pay more.

You may already have supplementary health insurance through a credit card, automobile club policy or employment health plan but you should check these carefully. Whatever policy you choose for your trip, carry details of it with you and documents showing that you are covered by a plan. You and your travelling companions should know how to contact your insurer, as should your travel agent and someone at home.

If you need medical attention while away, obtain a detailed invoice from the doctor or hospital for submission to the insurance company upon your return. Passengers who use wheelchairs or prosthetic devices should be sure these are included in any personal effects insurance they purchase. Pregnant women should check that complications arising from their condition are also covered. (Note: Most cruise lines will not accept women passengers who are in their seventh or later month of pregnancy.)

Health precautions

Vaccinations and medical attention

Vaccinations are rarely compulsory for holidays featured in cruise brochures, however immunisation against various infectious diseases is recommended for certain parts of the world. Consult your doctor for advice in this regard.

All large ships have a fully-equipped medical centre with a doctor and nurses. Their services are, however, outside the scope of NHS and passengers needing medical attention are billed at private rates which are added to their shipboard account. As mentioned, this invoice can be submitted to your insurance company upon your return home.

Seasickness

Motion sickness is not a widespread or prolonged problem with most passengers on a coastal cruise, however there are a number of remedies for those who are susceptible to this affliction. One is to wear special wrist bands, the balls of which rest on an acupressure point. Another option is to chew Meclizine tablets (often available at the ship's front office) or take Dramamine pills. It's best to take these pills ahead of time, before you feel too nauseous, and they may make you feel drowsy. A third solution is to wear a Scolpolamine patch behind one ear, but these have been known to produce side effects such as dizziness and blurred vision. Check first with your doctor before deciding on any medication.

Fresh air is one of the best antidotes to motion sickness, so stepping out on deck is often all that's needed to counter queasiness. Other simple remedies include sipping on ginger ale and nibbling on dry crackers

Typical cabins on Royal Caribbean Cruise Lines' latest megaship, Legend of the Seas. **Above** Standard outside stateroom. **Below** Standard inside stateroom.

Two types of cabin on Crystal Cruises' Crystal Harmony **Above** *Stateroom with verandah.* **Below** *De luxe stateroom.*

w ships. **Above** Launched in a blaze of
blicity in April 1995, P & O's newest ship, the
perliner Oriana.

ow A cutaway drawing reveals the scale of
 Royal Caribbean Cruise Lines megaship
end of the Seas.

Above *The shape of things to come. An artist's impression of Princess Cruises' Grand Princess, a 104,000-ton megaship due to be launched in 1997.* **Below** *New horizons. Hong Kong is one of the latest destinations offered to cruise passengers as the Far East is opened up for cruising.*

and an apple. Should you become concerned about your condition, simply visit the medical centre on board for professional attention.

What to pack

Clothes

If you are embarking on a fly/cruise, you will be limited by the airline to two suitcases and one carry-on bag per person. This same restriction usually applies to cruise passengers who are taking a land tour before or after their cruise. And even if you are boarding your ship in the UK for a round-trip cruise, the size of your cabin will determine how much luggage you should bring. People tend to travel lighter these days and with a bit of planning, everything you need for a one-to-two-week cruise can be fit into one or two suitcases.

Pack casual attire for daytime wear – both on board the ship and in port. The best approach is to dress in layers, especially in cooler climates, rather than pack bulky sweaters and coats. Mixing and matching is another key to stretching a travel wardrobe as is the use of accessories – scarves, jewellery, belts – that can be used to dress a basic outfit up or down, depending on the dress code in the dining room that evening.

For formal evenings on board the ship, the women wear gowns or cocktail dresses and the men favour black tie or dark suits. For informal evenings, the women wear dresses, skirts or slacks; the men wear jackets with either a shirt and tie or an open-necked shirt. Contrary to what many women expect, a cruise is not an on-going fashion parade among the passengers. Most people dress quite modestly apart from the few formal evenings when everyone seems to enjoy the opportunity to dress in their finest.

Footwear is also important. Your shoes and sandals should be comfortable, preferably with rubber soles to prevent slipping on the ship's decks, and leather uppers are preferable to canvas should they get wet. You may want to pack one pair of shoes for walking about on shore (where they may get dirty) and another pair for strolling about the ship. Give your shore shoes a good spray of all-weather protector before packing them. Headgear is another consideration. A wide-brimmed hat is recommended – one made of straw for the tropics or one of felt for cooler cruising areas. Sunglasses are also a necessity because even on cloudy days there will be glare off the water.

Most ships have laundrettes, which are either free or coin-operated, with soap automatically dispensed into the washer. An iron and iron-ing board are usually available. Passengers can also have their laundry done for them, as well as steam pressing and dry cleaning, all at an additional expense which is added to your shipboard account.

Other items

You may want to pack a small pair of binoculars for viewing the sights from the ship's deck. This is especially applicable on cruises that fea-ture frequent sightings of marine life such as those in Alaska.

Keep any prescribed medication in original, labelled containers and carry a doctor's prescription for any controlled drug. If you wear pre-scription eyeglasses or contact lenses, consider packing a spare pair. And keep all valuables (travellers cheques, camera, expensive jewellery) in your carry-on luggage as well as all prescription medicines and doc-umentation (passport, tickets, insurance policy).

The shops on board the large ships contain toiletries for passengers who forgot to pack an essential item. They also feature luxury goods – designer clothes, perfumes, jewellery, gifts and souvenirs – at duty free prices. (The QE2's Shopping Arcade even has a branch of Harrods on board.) Other products sold on board include film and duty free liquor.

Reading material

For passengers who didn't pack their own reading material, the ship's library will have magazines, paperbacks and books on a variety of sub-jects, both fiction and non-fiction. However, the librarian may not let you take out any guidebooks on the area you are cruising (so that all passengers have access to their information), so you may want to purchase beforehand an informative guidebook about the ports of call you will be visiting. Most cruise lines do provide some helpful port information either in the daily programme (slipped under your cabin door each day) or on a separate print-out that is often available at the Front Desk or Shore Excursion Office. There may also be a magazine in your cabin with information about the destinations you will be visiting in the course of your cruise.

Joining your cruise

This detail will be handled when you book your cruise, as most cruise lines offer special fares on flights and coach or rail transfers to the port at which you will be boarding your ship. Often a cruise line representative is on hand at the port city's airport to direct passengers to a waiting coach that will take them to the ship.

Once you reach the ship terminal, there will be cruise line representatives milling about to help passengers with any questions they might have. Passengers are processed quickly and efficiently once the ship is ready for embarkation and there's plenty of time for everyone to board. In fact, after the initial rush, most passengers do not have to wait.

Most cruise lines allow a few hours for embarkation. For instance, a ship leaving port at 5 p.m. will usually start boarding at about 2 p.m. (sometimes earlier) and no later than 3 p.m. Passengers are usually asked to be on board no later than an hour before the ship is due to sail.

If you decide to make your own travel arrangements and these involve an international flight, you may want to arrive at the port of embarkation the day before your cruise commences in case your flight is delayed and you face the nail-biting prospect of arriving too late to catch the ship. However, if you have booked an all-inclusive package with the cruise line, the time logistics will have been worked out for you.

Boarding the ship

When you arrive at the cruise terminal, your luggage (apart from carry-on bags) is handled by the longshoremen. You will have been provided with identification tags by the cruise line (part of your cruise ticket documentation) which must be attached to each piece of luggage. This tag identifies the ship on which you are sailing and contains your name and cabin number. Shortly after boarding, your luggage will be brought to your stateroom by your cabin steward or stewardess. He or she will be looking after your cabin and any requests you may have for the duration of the cruise.

A ship hums with activity just prior to sailing as passengers and their luggage are brought on board. Bon voyage celebrations often take place in the cabin if its occupants are lucky enough to have a chilled bottle of bubbly awaiting them. Some passengers, after locating their cabins, prefer to wander the decks and explore the ship. It should be noted that with security a high priority, most cruise lines no longer allow visitors on board their ships prior to departure.

On board

Your cabin

Unless you have booked a suite, your cabin will be smaller than a standard hotel room. It will, however, be kept spotless by your cabin steward or stewardess. Twice a day your cabin will be cleaned – once in the morning while you're at breakfast or ashore at a port of call, and again in the evening while you're at dinner. In cabins containing a couch that converts into a bed, this will be taken care of by your cabin steward who will turn your bed down each evening and make it up every morning. Twice daily any used towels will be replaced, waste-paper baskets emptied and the bathroom cleaned.

Storage space is somewhat limited but a basic cabin will contain a wardrobe for hanging dresses and suits, and drawers to hold your other clothes. Basic toiletries – such as soap, shampoo and hand lotion

– are usually provided, and a hairdryer may or may not be installed in the bathroom (you will be able to find this out at time of booking)

Beach towels for taking ashore will be provided by your steward on request, and deck towels can be found near the swimming pool. Any special requests, such as having your clothes laundered or dry cleaned, are handled by your cabin steward, who will collect and deliver your laundry.

Dinner reservations

Breakfast and lunch on board a cruise ship are usually open sittings, with meals served between set times. For dinner, however, you will be assigned a specific table at which the same waiter will serve you each evening.

When booking your cruise, you will be asked to indicate your preference for the first or second sitting at dinner, the size of table at which you would like to sit, and whether you want to be in a smoking or non-smoking section of the dining room. The earlier you book a cruise, the better your chance of being assigned your preferred sitting. (If you've booked onto a luxury ship, it will probably have only one sitting, and river cruises often have open sittings for all meals.)

Upon embarkation, you will find a note in your cabin confirming your table number and whether it's for the first or second sitting. If you want to change this, you should promptly visit the front office and submit your request which the maitre d'hotel will try to accommodate but cannot guarantee.

Some people prefer the first sitting because it gives them an entire evening afterwards to enjoy the stage show or other entertainment on board the ship. And if their appetite has returned by the end of the evening, they can stop by the midnight buffet. Early risers also tend to favour the first sitting.

On the other hand, the second sitting allows passengers plenty of time, after a full day in port, to freshen up and relax before dinner. Ships often depart a port at about 5 p.m. and passengers who choose the late sitting can linger on deck as the ship sails away and, if cruising in the tropics, they can enjoy the sunset before retiring to their cabins to wash and change for dinner.

The ship's staff

In the course of your cruise, you will come to recognise some of the ship's staff – especially those with high-profile positions such as the cruise director. He or she is in charge of entertainment on board the ship and serves as MC each evening for the stage acts in the theatre. Passengers interested in booking shore excursions will get to know the shore excursion manager, and of course your cabin steward and dining room steward are two people you will see every day. In charge of the large hotel staff is the ship's hotel manager whose responsibility it is to make sure every passenger is happy with the service they are receiving.

Separate from the hotel staff are the captain, chief engineer, and their officers and crew, who are responsible for the safe and efficient running of the ship. The captain is ultimately in charge of the entire ship and his role includes not only overseeing the officers on the bridge but fulfilling a social role on behalf of the cruise line. He and the hotel manager receive each and every passenger who attends the captain's welcoming cocktail party (usually the second night of a cruise) and he will occasionally dine with selected passengers at the captain's table.

Passengers with inquiries or seeking assistance can visit the Front Desk (also called the Purser's Office) where their needs will be handled by the appropriate staff member.

Lifeboat drill (mustering)

A mandatory safety drill involving all passengers is carried out on all ships within 24 hours of its departure. Many of the cruise lines conduct this drill before the ship even pulls away from the dock. Passengers are instructed over the loudspeaker system to don their lifejackets (which are stored in their cabin) and proceed to their appointed lifeboat station. Instructions are usually posted on the inside of the cabin door and your steward is always nearby to lend assistance.

Once all the ship's passengers have congregated on the boat deck at their designated stations (these are numbered), a member of the crew will check off each passenger's name to make sure everyone is in attendance. A demonstration then follows showing how the lifeboats will be lowered into the water in the unlikely event of an abandon-ship emergency. Once this procedure is finished, (the entire drill takes about 20 minutes) passengers are then allowed to return to their cabins, remove their lifejackets and stow them in their proper place. It's now time for everyone to completely relax and do whatever they desire which, for most people, is standing at the rail and waving to bystanders on shore as the ship eases away from the dock and the cruise begins.

Shipboard account

Most ships are cashless societies in which passengers simply sign for incidental expenses such as drinks in a bar, dry cleaning services, massages, facials and haircuts. Even purchases in the onboard shops are signed to your cabin. At the end of the cruise, an itemised statement of account will be delivered to your cabin. This account can, on most cruise lines, be settled by credit card, traveller's cheque, personal cheque or cash. You can confirm this beforehand either by reading the fine print at the back of the cruise brochure or perusing the package of information that arrives with your cruise ticket.

Tipping

Although tipping is a cruising tradition, no passenger is obliged to hand out tips at the end of a cruise. However, most are more than happy with the service they receive and enjoy rewarding the people who have served them. Your cruise line will provide you with guidelines on how much to tip various staff, but a general rule is to tip your cabin steward £2 or £3 per passenger for each day of the voyage, your table steward the same amount, and his assistant £1 per passenger per day. Your wine steward should receive 10 to 15 percent of your total wine bill, although some cruise lines include gratuities for bar staff and wine waiters in all beverage bills. Tips are usually given the last night of the cruise. Some cruise lines will include the cost of tips in your cruise ticket so that you needn't concern yourself with this.

Going ashore

At each port of call the ship will either dock or anchor. Most cruise lines are willing to pay the dock fees rather than anchor, which entails lowering the tenders (small boats) for transporting passengers ashore. Generally speaking, ships anchor when there is no dock space left or proper dock facilities do not exist at a particular port. Dock space is reserved in advance by each cruise line and it's possible to find out, either by reading the cruise brochure or asking your travel agent, at which ports the ship will be docking versus anchoring.

When your ship pulls into a port at which it drops anchor, there will be a minor delay in getting ashore. Passengers who have booked soon-to-begin shore excursions are transported ashore first, followed by those who have proceeded to a designated area to obtain a number and, upon that number being called, are allowed to board a tender. However, because the ships usually pull into port early in the morning, most people don't even notice the delay because they're still in the dining room having breakfast or in their cabins enjoying a leisurely start to the day when the tenders begin heading ashore. By the time many of the passengers are ready to go ashore, there is no longer any wait involved.

Getting back to the ship is simply a matter of returning to the dock at which you disembarked from the tender. A ship's officer is stationed there throughout the day, supervising the coming and going of tenders. You can catch a ride back to the ship at any time during the its stay in port and although queues tend to form in the last hour that the tenders are running prior to the ship's departure, these do move quickly. For tardy passengers who return to the tender dock in time to see their ship raising its anchor and steaming away from port, a dock worker may be able to radio the ship. The officer on the bridge will either lower a tender to retrieve the stranded passengers or a pilot boat might be engaged to whisk the latecomers out to the ship while it waits. The only penalty for such tardiness is extreme embarrassment as people watch from the rail while these wayward passengers are brought on board and the ship can finally get underway. However, anyone who fails to return to the ship after it has left port, is responsible for any costs incurred in getting to the next port of call to reconnect with the cruise.

Phoning home

Passengers wishing to place a ship-to-shore telephone call need only contact the ship's radio office and request that either a satellite call be placed or a radio call. Satellite telephone calls are the most convenient (and expensive) option, providing a high-quality connection and complete privacy. Radio calls are less expensive than satellite calls but are not private, can be time consuming to place, and may fade in and out. If the call is not urgent, you may want to wait and place it from a land-based phone at the next port of call. The new pre-paid telephone calling cards offer an easy way for passengers to place long distance calls while in port. These cards allow the user to make international and domestic calls from any touchtone phone. They are sold on board a few ships, namely those in the Princess Cruises fleet, but some other travel agents can sell you one before you leave the UK.

Holiday photos

A pleasant aspect of cruise travel is the presence of professional photographers on board the ship. They are there to capture highlights of each passenger's cruise experience such as embarkation, the captain's welcoming cocktail party and formal nights in the dining room. The ship's photographers also mingle with passengers throughout the days and evenings, capturing happy and impromptu moments on film. All of their prints are displayed in the ship's photo gallery where passengers can view them at their leisure and order any they may want to take home at the end of the cruise.

Of course, many travellers are keen to take their own photographs, especially at the various ports of call. The serious camera buff will need no advice but for those of you who are point-and-shoot photographers, here are a few tips. First, if you are taking a brand new camera on your trip, shoot and develop a roll of film at home beforehand to make sure the camera works properly and that you understand all its features. Second, pack more film than you anticipate using rather than waste holiday time looking for shops that sell fresh film at reasonable prices. For automatic cameras, 200-ASA print film is probably your best choice for all-around lighting conditions. Make sure you've got fresh batteries in the camera and remember to have fun with your picture taking. Be spontaneous and creative rather than analytical when framing a shot. The subject matter should fill the frame so move in closer if there's a lot of superfluous space in your viewfinder.

Disembarkation

On the final night of your cruise you will probably be asked to leave your packed and labelled suitcases outside your cabin door before retiring for the night. This is standard procedure because disembarkation often takes place the next morning. It's therefore important to once again keep all valuables and travel documents with you in your carry-on bag, as well as the outfit you plan to wear the next day. Many a cruise director has a story to tell about passengers who pack all of their clothes before going to bed and realise the next morning that they had only their pyjamas to wear off the ship!

Assuming you have kept clothes to wear the last morning of your cruise, you can usually enjoy a leisurely albeit early breakfast before disembarkation announcements begin over the PA system. Most large ships disembark passengers in groups – those with early flights to catch disembark first – and the last batch of passengers have usually left the ship by mid-morning.

Your luggage will be waiting for you in the cruise terminal where you pick it up before proceeding through Customs and Immigration (if returning home) or boarding a coach for transfer to the airport and your flight home.

7 New ships, new horizons

New ships

The 1990s have been one of busiest decades this century for passenger ship building. Some of the largest ships ever built are being launched and they keep getting bigger, with ships over 100,000 tons just around the corner.

This rapid pace of ship construction is expected to continue almost to the end of the decade. Over 20 new ships have either been contracted or are planned for construction to the end of 1998. And this is good news for holidaymakers planning to take a cruise because it means greater diversity in ship selection, better choice of itineraries and competitive fares as cruise lines vie for passengers and market share.

The ship of the future has already been revealed by some recent launches. Ships are being built higher, especially in the stern area, to provide greater interior space and cabins on most new ships are being located more forward and aft than even a few years ago. As a result, new ships have the deserved complaint they are box-like in appearance. On the plus side, these new ships are providing a higher percentage of outside cabins – especially ones with balconies. Also, the trend is to provide more boat for your money. Public areas such as lounges, restaurants, theatres and viewing areas are all becoming larger. And since these areas are open to all, every passenger, no matter what level of cabin, benefits.

Naval architects have acknowledged that ships will probably not get much larger than 100,000 tons (or 3000-passenger capacity). The reason is a sharp decline in efficiency of design beyond this size – the ship ends up with too much interior space which would have to be filled with inside cabins (something many passengers don't want) or with low-revenue-producing public areas.

Each cruise line has its own approach to the motif and finished quality of the ship's interior. For instance, Holland America Line uses its Dutch naval tradition as a theme throughout the fleet and employs brass, teak and 'nautical-realism' artwork to complement the colour and decor of each new ship. The result presents the passenger with a feel or ambiance unique to Holland America. Celebrity Cruises uses contemporary art and stronger colours to impart an aura of modern luxury. This concept of creating a pleasant ambiance through thematic decor is recognised by most cruise lines as a critical ingredient in new ship design.

A recent feature on cruise ships is that of the glass-domed atrium, which creates the effect of bringing light deep into the central part of the ship. This architectural centrepiece also serves as a point of reference, making it easier for passengers to orient themselves with what at first seems like an immense resort.

Royal Caribbean Cruise Lines' *Legend of the Seas* contains a remarkable example of this modern design concept. The ship has a seven-deck glass-walled atrium and over two acres of glass, making for a well-lit ship with numerous vantage points for viewing the scenery. This megaship also features RCCL's trademark nightclub/observatory, the Viking Lounge, which is wrapped around the funnel and a two-storey dining room with almost no obstructions to the outside views. The *Legend* also has the world's first floating 18-hole miniature golf course which has proved to be very popular despite the obvious water trap.

These sorts of innovations reflect the efforts of the cruise industry to provide more passengers with more choice in a range of areas such as entertainment, food, recreation and family facilities. The cruise companies are well aware that in addition to being a good hotel, a ship must have a selection of activities for all age groups in order to compare well with the better resorts of the world.

For example, P & O's new liner *Oriana,* launched in April 1995, has nine bars, five dance floors, three swimming pools, two spas, three restaurants, a casino, a health centre with gymnasium, a deck tennis court, a children's paddling pool, a night nursery, teen rooms, video games rooms, a cinema, beauty salons, shops and a theatre. It also has a medical centre, a library and writing rooms.

The efforts of cruise companies to offer greater flexibility is evident in most of the new designs of this decade and is made possible to some extent by the fact the ships are larger and have less people on board. Ships built in the 1950s and 1960s tended to accommodate more people per ton of ship. This is referred to as the passenger/space ratio and is calculated by dividing the total tonnage by the passenger capacity. This ratio began to improve over the following two decades and has accelerated in the 1990s. On average, a ship of this decade will have about 30% more room per passenger than a ship built in the 50s or 60s. This is a trend which appears to be here to stay.

Two major cruise lines recently announced contracts for new 'super-megaships' over 100,000 tons. These ships could have handled 4000 passengers quite easily in the days when there were different classes of passengers but, in the modern era of one-class ships, they will be designed to accommodate about 2600 passengers. For reference purposes the *Titanic,* largest ship of its time, was just 46,000 tons with a passenger capacity of 2500, and the *Queen Elizabeth,* which was the largest ship ever (displacing 83,673 tons) had a passenger capacity of 2300 – although during the War she transported over 11,000 troops at a time.

Carnival Cruise Line plans to launch *Carnival Destiny* in 1996 and it will be the largest ship ever built, at what is expected to be about 105,000 tons. Constructed at a cost of over $400 million, this will be a 12-deck ship with some interesting innovations. For example, most ships, even the megaships, have one large dining room. The *Destiny* will have two double-deck dining rooms with glass chandeliers and two grand staircases. And passengers who are seated in the middle of the dining room will, thanks to a raised floor, still have an ocean view.

But it will probably be the launch of Princess Cruise's *Grand Princess* in 1997 that will cause the biggest stir. Expected to be about 104,000 tons, this ship has been loaded with an array of technological distractions sure to keep even the most hyperactive passenger pacified. This includes a motion-based virtual reality theatre (where did the actors go?), interactive technology such as a golf driving range that will allow passengers to play on some of the world's best-known courses and a 'blue screen' room which will give passengers the chance to star in their own video production so they don't have to go to the virtual reality theatre. Perhaps the most interesting design feature of the *Grand Princess* is a nightclub at the stern of the ship, suspended like a huge wing above the other decks. This will be 15 storeys (or decks) above sea level and give passengers an experience that cruising is really all about – a wonderful view of the sea and passing scenery.

New horizons

Cruising has enjoyed over a decade of phenomenal growth which has been a boon to many small cities and ports of the world. However, because over 75 per cent of passengers are repeat cruisers, there is a growing demand for new ports and itineraries. Some ports, especially in the Caribbean, are close to saturation point in the number of people they can handle, so there is an added impetus for cruise lines to find new attractions for their loyal client base. And the ports are responding.

From the east coast of Canada to the exotic Far East, ports are courting the cruise lines in an effort to be included in their new itineraries. Even the Caribbean's list of ports has expanded significantly in the last five years and cruise company executives are looking at other ports as potential new stops in the future. One Caribbean island long overdue for the return of tourism is Cuba. Many in the industry see the cruise ships stopping here once normalisation of relations with the United States occurs. Cuba would require large investments in port facilities to handle the docking of big ships and the large volume of passengers, but some of this funding would no doubt come from the cruise companies.

The cruise lines are also looking at extending their length of stay at popular ports. Most ships remain in a port from early morning until late afternoon before steaming off to the next one. While this is adequate for some ports of call, the cruise lines have found there is a desire on the part of passengers to stay longer at certain popular destinations. Bermuda is one example of people specifically taking this cruise so they can leisurely explore the islands for three or four days while using the ship as a hotel. Some cruise lines see Barbados and the Cayman Islands as other potential 'extended time' stops meriting an extra day for passengers to completely experience the island.

Extended visits at popular destinations could become very big in Europe. According to the World Tourism Organisation, based in Madrid, land-based travel on the Continent is destined to become a lot more crowded. Tourists may have to make reservations to climb the Eiffel Tower, or book months ahead to see museums and monuments. Environmental concerns could prevent the expansion of Mediterranean resorts at which natural scenery is a major attraction, thus making them unable to cope with the growing tourist demand.

All of this continues to give cruise travel an increasing edge. Passengers' shore excursions are contracted by the cruise lines months in advance of their visit. And ports in the future may see the cruise ship as the ideal way to handle tourists and still benefit from the trade. Cruise ships don't alter the landscape – there is no need for large infrastructures such as monolithic hotels, car rental agencies and parking lots. Most cruise passengers tour the local sights on foot, by shuttle bus or take a coach tour, and of course the ship is their hotel. The only thing left behind by cruise ships is the money spent by its passengers.

For the traveller of the future, cruising may be the best way to see a busy city where hotel and food costs can be astronomical. The bustle of a city is great for a day or two but the space, comfort and relaxed pace on a ship make it a welcome retreat that holidaymakers can look forward to at the end of a long day of sightseeing.

Most areas of the world have opened up to tourists and cruise itineraries will keep expanding to take in more and different ports. Some cruise lines will mix a bit of adventure with an otherwise mainstream cruise to give passengers a unique voyage. One recent example is Crystal Cruises' 'Mysteries of the Amazon' cruise, during which the ship actually journeys 700 miles up the Amazon River, stopping at ports along the way. Holland America offers a circumnavigation of South America and another example of creative itinerary planning is the 'Solar Eclipse Cruise' that Orient Lines promoted for October 1995 in the South China Sea.

Perhaps of all world destinations the Far East has the most potential, simply because there are so many ports and such a diversity of cultures. The importance of the cruise industry to this area is evident in the investment many ports have made in recent years to improve dock facilities. And it seems to be paying off – Singapore, Hong Kong, Indonesia, Malaysia, Thailand, China and even Vietnam all draw regular visits by cruise ships.

As more people see the advantage of slowing down and seeing the world from the water, more variety will be offered to the public. In America river cruising is enjoying a surge in popularity Mark Twain would have been proud to see. Regular 11-night sailings up and down the big Mississippi by a number of paddlewheelers, including the new 436-passenger *American Queen*, have become a popular way to see this great waterway.

As the 20th century draws to a close, one of the oldest modes of transport appears poised to become the travel holiday of the future.

8 Booking your cruise

Armed with information contained in the preceding chapters of this book, you will be well on your way to choosing the cruise best suited to your holiday plans. This chapter will help you towards finding a specific cruise holiday and provide guidelines on how to book a cruise. To make the process a little easier, we have also provided a cruise selection chart on pp. 138–139 which, used in conjunction with the notes in this chapter and the fuller information in the rest of the book, should assist you in pinpointing the right kind of cruise for you.

The role of the travel agent

The first step is to visit a reliable travel agent, one which belongs to the Association of British Travel Agents (ABTA). Thomas Cook has been in business since 1841 and books more cruises than any other British agent. Its staff are trained professionals who have immediate access to any information you may request regarding the various cruise companies, and can advise on any special offers available for the dates and cruise line you wish to book.

Feel free to wander into any Thomas Cook shop and ask whatever questions you might have about cruising. And don't worry about sounding uninformed – the majority of people know very little about shipboard travel and what a cruising holiday entails. A good way to get a better impression of cruises is to ask your travel agent to show you a video taken on board one of the ships so that you can see just how large and spacious modern cruise liners are and the range of activities that can be enjoyed on board.

Thomas Cook shops are well stocked with brochures on various cruise lines and you can take a selection of these home to leaf through at your leisure. The photos inside will give you a fairly good impression of the clientele each line appeals to and the atmosphere found on board. (Bear in mind, however, that professional models are often used for these photos; you needn't worry about competing, because few real-life passengers look as glamorous as those depicted in the brochures!) Jot down any questions you would like to ask your travel agent about a particular cruise line and/or cruising region.

Cost

The first question on most people's minds is 'how much does a cruise cost?' Below is a rough guideline on the sort of cruise you can expect for the money you are prepared to spend. Factors determining the cost are the destination, the length of the cruise holiday, the type of cruise line and the grade of cabin. The prices quoted are per person based on double occupancy and include accommodation, meals and entertainment. These general prices also allow for airfares, port taxes and transfers. They do not include onboard purchases such as drinks or gifts.

£399–£1000
Basic inside cabin – sometimes better on 3★ and 4★ ships. Holidays of 4–7 days. Ex-UK, and some fly/cruises to the Mediterranean and Caribbean.

£1000–£2000
Basic cabin on 3★ to 4★+ range of ships – depending on length of cruise. Some 5★ cruises available. Holidays of 7–10 days or more. Ex-UK, fly/cruises to Mediterranean and Caribbean. Some 7-day fly/cruises to Alaska and even some Far East and South Pacific fly/cruises.

£2000–£3000
Better cabin selection – outside, some with balcony – on a good selection of 4–5★ ships. Holidays of 10+ days. Ex-UK, fly/cruises to Mediterranean and Caribbean. 10+ days fly/cruises to Alaska and South Pacific fly/cruises.

£3000–£5000
The better cabins on the better ships would be available in this price range choosing from a good selection of 4★+ and 5★ ships. Holidays of 10–14 days or more with cruises to most destinations. Some extended cruises of over 20 days also available.

£5000+
Upper-grade cabin selection, on 4★+ and 5★ ships. Cruise length generally 14+ days – range of extended cruises available of 20 -30+ days. Worldwide destinations.

When and where to go, and for how long

Once you have determined your travel budget, the next questions are ones you must ask yourself: Where would you like to go? What time of the year would you like to go on holiday? How long a holiday would you like to take? You may already know what part of the world you want to see. However, if you're open to all sorts of suggestions, Chapter 4, *Ports of Call,* may help you decide where you would most like to visit.

Some of the popular cruising areas are seasonal while others can be cruised throughout the year. The Caribbean can be visited by cruise ships year round although January through March are its high-season months when the weather is at its best and visitors come to escape the winter weather at home. Spring, summer and autumn are the most popular cruising seasons in the Mediterranean and cruises to Scandinavia and Alaska run throughout the summer. The Canary Islands are a popular winter destination for cruises, as are the South Pacific and Far East.

The more popular the cruising region, the more choice there is in terms of cruise lines and lengths of cruises available. For instance, Caribbean cruises range from three nights to two weeks. (A glance at Chapter 5 will show you the variety of choices available.) If you prefer to avoid travelling by plane, then an ex-UK cruise would be your best choice. If you are prone to seasickness, a cruise in a sheltered coastal area, such as Alaska's Inside Passage, or a river cruise, is recommended.

Which cruise line and which ship

Once you have determined your budget, destination, time and duration of travel, the next question is, 'Which cruise line?' Although most cruise passengers spend a great deal of their holiday time on shore exploring the ports of call, the ship itself is an important part of the holiday. On a typical ten-day Caribbean cruise, for example, three full days are spent at sea. So it's important that you choose a ship with an atmosphere you enjoy. Your travel agent will be able to help you here, as will the description of the various cruise lines in Chapter 5. Opposite is a sample of ships in the various categories. (For a description of these categories, see the *Glossary of cruising terms* on p. 140).

Perhaps one approach is to consider the type of holiday you are seeking, i.e. one that is active, restful, adventurous, cultural or educational? If you want lots of physical activity and excitement, then a cruise line that attracts a young active crowd may be what you want. If you have a young family, choose a cruise line with a nursery and lots of supervised activities for children. (Some cruise lines do not accept children under six months of age.) If you are looking forward to peace and quiet, or perhaps a romantic interlude, then ask about cruise lines with a more sedate and relaxed atmosphere where you can unwind at your leisure.

Examples of cruise lines that attract a young crowd are Carnival, Cunard *Countess* and *Dynasty*, Norwegian Cruise Lines and Royal Caribbean Cruise Lines. Cruise ships that appeal to young families include the Carnival ships, P & O's *Canberra*, Princess Cruises' *Star Princess* and *Sky Princess* and Royal Caribbean Cruise Line's fleet. Ships that offer a more relaxed and refined cruise culture tend to be the 4★+ and 5★ ships. Some examples of these are the fleets of Celebrity Cruises, Crystal Cruises, Cunard's *Sagafjord* and *Vistafjord*, Holland America Line and some of the Princess Cruises ships. Some ships have such a wide range of facilities and grades of cabin, they appeal to all types of passengers, two examples being the *QE2* and *Oriana*.

8 Booking your cruise

Luxury Class (5★)

Crystal Cruises	*Crystal Harmony, Crystal Symphony*
Cunard	*QE2, Royal Viking Sun, Sagafjord, Vistafjord, Sea Goddess I and II*
Seabourn Cruise Line	*Seabourn Pride, Seabourn Spirit*
Silversea Cruises	*Silver Cloud, Silver Wind*

Upper Mainstream (4★+)

Celebrity Cruises	*Zenith, Horizon, Meridian*
Costa Cruises	*Costa Romantica, Costa Classica*
Cunard	*Cunard Dynasty*
Holland America Line	*Statendam, Ryndam, Maasdam, Noordam, Nieuw Amsterdam, Westerdam*
P & O	*Oriana, Victoria*
Princess Cruises	*Sun Princess, Royal Princess, Regal Princess, Crown Princess, Star Princess*
Royal Caribbean Cruise Line	*Majesty of the Seas, Monarch of the Seas, Legend of the Seas, Splendour of the Seas, Sovereign of the Seas, Nordic Empress*

Mainstream (4★)

Carnival Cruises	*Ecstasy, Imagination*
Costa Cruises	*Costa Marina, Costa Allegra*
Cunard	*Cunard Countess*
Fred Olsen Cruises	*Black Prince*
Norwegian Cruise Lines	*Dreamward, Windward, Norway, Seaward*
Orient Lines	*Marco Polo*
P & O	*Canberra*
Princess Cruises	*Golden Princess, Island Princess, Sky Princess*
Royal Caribbean Cruise Line	*Sun Viking, Song of America.*

Budget (3★)

Airtours	*Carousel, Seawing*
CTC	*Sothern Cross*
Regency Cruise Lines	*Regent Sun, Regent Rainbow*
Thomson Cruises	*Sapphire*

Expedition

Alaska Sightseeing Cruise West	*Spirit of Alaska*
Clipper Cruise Lines	*World Discoverer, Yorktown Clipper*
Orient Lines	*Marco Polo* (has conventional and expedition cruises)
Star Clipper	
Swan Hellenic	*Minerva, Spice Islander, Island Explorer*

Specialist cruise lines aim to enrich your knowledge or interest in a particular field and have an expedition-like approach. The voyages of these ships will have a cultural focus. River cruises are also culturally biased.

When deciding on a specific ship, you should be aware that the newer ships (those built in the late 80s and 90s) will often have more public space and sometimes larger cabins, including ones specifically designed for passengers with wheelchairs. Older ships will have smaller windows or portholes and less public area; however they often have loyal followings due to their traditional charm and an intimacy that new ships sometimes lack. The older ships also have more single cabins than do contemporary ships. Examples of classic liners are Cunard's *QE2*, P & O's *Canberra*, Norwegian Cruise Line's *Norway* and Holland America Line's *Rotterdam*. Bigger does not always mean better by the way. Some of the highest rated ships in the world are small, such as those of Cunard Royal Viking.

Your cabin

It's important that you are happy with your cabin because once you're on board the ship it is extremely difficult, often impossible, to move to another cabin. Ships are often fully booked and the highest grade cabins are usually occupied, leaving little selection for a passenger disgruntled with the accommodation. For some people, the size and amenities of their cabin are of little concern, because they plan to spend most of their time in the ship's public areas enjoying the facilities. For others who prefer to retreat to their cabin at frequent intervals, a larger cabin is often a priority. Your travel agent should understand what your expectations are regarding accommodation and be able to tell you exactly what you are getting in terms of cabin space – its size, bed arrangement and bathroom facilities. However, before placing too much emphasis on the grade of cabin you choose, bear in mind that everyone on board a ship enjoys the same cruise experience regardless of their private accommodation.

Illustrated opposite are typical cutaway cabin layouts, in this case taken from Holland America Line's brochure. Each cruise line brochure contains diagrams of the ship's decks, with all cabins numbered and coded

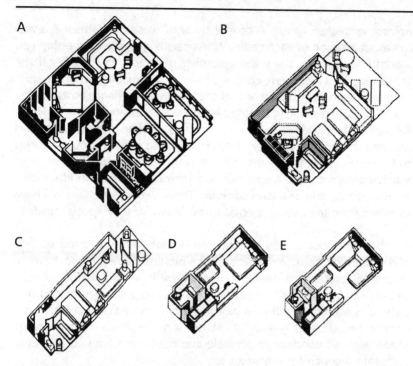

A Penthouse Suite, Navigation Deck. **B** Deluxe Suite, Navigation Deck. **C** Deluxe outside rooms, Navigation and Verandah Decks. **D** Large outside rooms, Verandah, Lower Promenade, Main and A Decks. **E** Large inside rooms, Navigation, Lower Promenade, Main and A Decks.

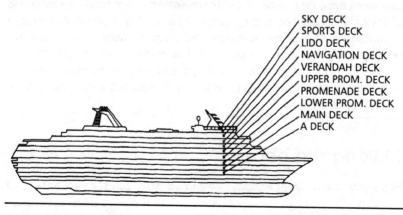

SKY DECK
SPORTS DECK
LIDO DECK
NAVIGATION DECK
VERANDAH DECK
UPPER PROM. DECK
PROMENADE DECK
LOWER PROM. DECK
MAIN DECK
A DECK

according to their grade. A careful study of these diagrams will reveal the exact location of each cabin. When deciding where on the ship you would like to sleep, there are a number of factors to consider. If the ship's motion is a concern, choose a cabin in the middle part of the ship. Cabins located near the aft end of the ship will experience more engine vibration during docking procedures than those located forward. Those located far forward will experience the most motion if the ship's bow is plowing through a heavy sea. If you have young children, you may want to locate yourself close to the ship's nursery. And passengers with physical handicaps should try to position themselves near the lifts rather than at the far end of a long corridor. (Those with wheelchairs will have to select from the cabins specifically designed for their special needs.)

The higher decks usually contain the largest cabins, located outside and often with balconies. These are the highest grade (i.e. most expensive) cabins. The next deck down will have lower grades of cabins – usually smaller and with fewer facilities such as a shower instead of a bath, a window instead of a balcony. The lower passenger decks will contain the cheaper grades of cabins. Some of these will be located inside with no window or porthole and may contain a bed that converts into a couch for daytime use.

When booking your accommodation, you can reserve a specific cabin or you can book a level of cabin at a guaranteed rate with the possibility that you may be upgraded. To take advantage of upgrades, it's best to book well in advance. A cruise line may sometimes upgrade you to a more expensive cabin if it subsequently receives bookings in excess of the cabins available at the lower price level. Many people like to take advantage of these free upgrades and do so by booking at a guaranteed rate. However, others prefer to know exactly where on the ship their cabin is located and feel this is more important than being moved into a larger cabin that might not be ideally situated according to their personal preferences.

Making the booking

People who plan their holidays well in advance can take advantage of the cruise lines' early booking discounts. These discounts are especially generous in popular cruising areas being serviced by a high number of cruise lines. When there are more berths available than passengers filling them, the market is said to be in a state of over-capacity and this will prompt the cruise companies to discount their fares in an effort to fill all their cabins. Make sure that the travel agent handling your cruise reservation and deposit is a member of The Association of British Travel Agents (ABTA) which will ensure the protection of your money.

Travel agents require a deposit to confirm your reservation, with the balance due about 60 days prior to your departure date. If you are making a last-minute booking, the entire fare must be paid in full. The major cruise lines are bonded members of the Passenger Shipping Association and your money will be protected. Should you wish to cancel your booking after the balance has been paid in full, a cancellation charge will be deducted from your refund. For example, if you cancel six weeks prior to sailing, the cruise company's cancellation charge might be 20% of the total fare; if you cancel 15 days prior to sailing, the charge could be as much as 75%; and should you fail to embark on the cruise, you will probably have to forfeit 100% of your cruise fare. The brochure from which you book your cruise will explain the conditions imposed by that cruise line in detail. A cruise company's booking conditions are stated near the back of its brochures. You should read these pages carefully. Port taxes are sometimes additional and these vary from cruise line to cruise line, but generally speaking they are between £50 to £100 per passenger.

If you plan to book a complete package through your travel agent, such as air flights, overnight hotel accommodation, transfers and overland tours, all such arrangements must be made when you book your cruise. Optional shore excursions at the ports of call can be booked once you are on the cruise.

When making your cruise booking, be sure to indicate your preferred sitting for dinner (first or second), the size of table at which you would like to sit (i.e. table for two, four, six or eight), whether you want to sit in a smoking or non-smoking section, and any special dietary requirements you may have (i.e. diabetic, vegetarian, kosher).

Cruise selector

Use this chart to guide you to the cruises that best meet your requirements and budget. Use Boxes 1 to 7 to help you decide on your preferences in the major considerations when choosing a cruise – how much you want to spend, when and where you want to go, etc. – and then check these against the list of lines and ships in Box 8 to narrow the field down to the cruise possibilities you should look at first. Remember that none of these lists contain all the possibilities; at this stage you should consult your ABTA travel agent, who will be able to guide you to the best choices available, any special deals, new ships and new itineraries, etc. By checking through this selection guide first (it may help to circle your preferences in each box) you will be able to give your agent a better idea of which cruise brochures to explore.

1 Length of cruise
3 nights
4 nights–1 week
1–2 weeks
2 weeks–1 month
Over 1 month

2 Price (per person)
Under £500
£500–£1000
£1–2000
£2–3000
£3–5000
£5000+

3 Type of cabin
Basic inside
Outside
Outside with balcony
Mini-suite
Suite

4 Rating of cruise line or ship
Budget 3★
Mainstream 4★
Upper mainstream 4★+
Luxury 5★
River cruise ship
Expedition ship

5 Itinerary type
Fly-cruise
Ex-UK (if you don't like flying)

6 Atmosphere/facilities (see symbols in Box 8)

Lots of activities	A
Ideal for children	C
Educational/cultural	E
Ideal for over-50s	O
Peace and quiet	P
Single cabins	S
Young passengers	Y

7 Travel season and destination

Winter	Spring
Caribbean	Caribbean
Canaries/Madeira	Mediterranean
South Pacific/Far East	Canaries/Madeira
River cruise – Nile	River cruise – Nile
Round the world	River cruise – Europe/USA
	Transatlantic
	Round the world

Summer	Autumn
Bermuda	Bermuda
Mediterranean	Mediterranean
Scandinavia	River cruise –Nile
Alaska & Western Canada	River cruise – Europe/USA
River cruise – Europe/USA	Canada & Eastern coast USA

Cruise selector

8

Cruise line/ship	Rating	Itinerary type	Atmosphere & facilities	Destinations (but check with your travel agent)
Airtours	3★	Fly-cruise		Mediterranean
Alaska Sightseeing	Expedition	Fly-cruise	A, E	Alaska, Canada
Carnival	4★	Fly-cruise	A, C, Y	Caribbean, Mexico
Celebrity Cruises	4★+	Fly-cruise	C, O, P	Caribbean, Alaska
Costa Cruises	4★/4★+	Fly-cruise/ex-UK	C, O, P	Caribbean, Mediterranean, Scandinavia
Crystal Cruises	5★	Fly-cruise/ex-UK	A, O, P	Worldwide
Cunard: QE2	4★+/5★+	Fly-cruise/ex-UK	A, C, E	Transatlantic, World
Cunard: RV Sun, Sea Goddess I & II	5★+	Fly-cruise	A, O, P	Caribbean, Mediterranean, World
Cunard: Sagafjord, Vistafjord	5★	Fly-cruise/ex-UK	O, P, S	Mediterranean, Caribbean, Alaska
Cunard Countess/Dynasty	4★	Fly-cruise/ex-UK	A, Y	Mediterranean, Caribbean, Alaska
CTC	3★	Fly-cruise/ex-UK	C, S	Scandinavia, Caribbean, Mediterranean
Fred Olsen Lines	3★	Fly-cruise/ex-UK	A, S	Scandinavia, Mediterranean
Holland America Line: Rotterdam	4★+	Fly-cruise	O, P, S	Alaska, World
Holland America Line: All other ships	4★+	Fly-cruise/ex-UK	A, O, P	Alaska, Caribbean, Europe
KD River Cruises	River	Fly-cruise	E	Europe, Nile
Norwegian Cruise Lines:				
Dreamward, Norway, Windward	4★+	Fly-cruise	A, C, Y	Caribbean, Alaska
Norwegian Cruise Lines: *Seaward, Starward*	4★	Fly-cruise	A, C, Y	Caribbean
Orient Lines	4★	Fly-cruise	A, E, S	Far East, Alaska
P & O: *Canberra*	4★	Fly-cruise/ex-UK	C, S, Y	Mediterranean, Scandinavia
P & O: *Oriana*	4★+	Fly-cruise/ex-UK	A, C	Mediterranean, Caribbean, World
P & O: *Victoria*	4★+	Fly-cruise	O, P	Mediterranean, Scandinavia
Princess Cruises:				
Royal, Crown, Regal, Sun, Star	4★	Fly-cruise/ex-UK	A, O, P	Alaska, Caribbean, Mediterranean
Princess Cruises: *Golden, Sky, Pacific*	4★	Fly-cruise	A, O, P	Alaska, Caribbean, South Pacific
Royal Caribbean Cruise Line:				
Sun Viking, Song of America	4★	Fly-cruise	A, C, Y	Far East, Caribbean
Royal Caribbean Cruise Line: All other ships	4★+	Fly-cruise/ex-UK	A, C, Y	Caribbean, Alaska
Swan Hellenic	River/Expedition	Fly-cruise	E	Mediterranean, Europe
Thomas Cook Holidays	River	Fly-cruise		Nile
Thomson	3★	Fly-cruise		

Glossary of cruising terms

All the technical terms and cruise jargon which have been used in this book are collected and explained here for handy reference. Although there is no need to master all the vocabulary of the cruise trade, it is useful to understand some of the more common phrases when consulting brochures or discussing your requirements with your travel agent.

Aft Near or in the **stern** (rear) of the ship.

Cabin Private accommodation on board a ship is called a *cabin* or *stateroom*. Large cabins are often referred to as *suites*. An *outside cabin* is one with a porthole, window or balcony. An *inside cabin* has no porthole or window but there is sometimes a curtain covering one wall to provide the illusion of there being a window behind it.

Companionway An inside stairway.

Crew-to-passenger ratio This to some extent determines the level of service on board a ship – the more crew per passenger the better the service is likely to be. For example, a ship carrying 500 crew and 1000 passengers has a ratio of 1 crew member for every 2 passengers. Note: The passenger capacity quoted in this book for each ship is based on double occupancy of all cabins.

Cruise-only fare The actual cost of the cruise excluding all extras such as taxes, port charges, air fares, tips, and so on.

Double occupancy The cabin rate per person for cabins capable of accommodating two people. Higher, **single occupancy**, rates are charged when a two-person cabin is only occupied by one passenger.

Embarkation Entering or boarding the ship; leaving the ship is **disembarkation**.

Flag of convenience A ship is often registered outside its country of administration and this is done for financial reasons. Thus a ship with its head office in London might be registered in, for example, Liberia, Panama or the

Glossary of cruising terms

Bahamas, but still be very British in terms of its atmosphere and clientele. The location of a cruise company's head office is the best indicator of the passenger nationality it attracts.

Flagship The best ship in a cruise line's fleet, or sometimes the oldest or the newest.

Fly/cruise A package which combines air travel to and/or from the port of embarkation with the cruise trip itself.

Forward Near or in the **bow** (front) of the ship.

Inside cabin See **Cabin**.

Itinerary The exact dates and route of a cruise, including port of embarkation and disembarkation, and all ports of call visited in between. From one year to the next cruise lines are constantly fine-tuning and altering the itineraries they offer and those described in this book are what is currently being offered. To check a ship's future itineraries, talk to your travel agent.

Knots The speed of a ship calculated by distance travelled, in nautical miles, in the space of an hour. A nautical mile is equal to 1.15 land miles.

Lido deck An upper stern deck containing a pool and restaurant.

Line voyages Cruises that involve the passenger in at least one flight to the port of embarkation or disembarkation – for example, a cruise from Southampton to the Mediterranean with a return flight home from Athens.

Lower bed An ordinary bed at normal height.

Open sitting Free access to tables in the dining room, as opposed to pre-assigned tables.

Outside cabin See **Cabin**.

Port The left side of the ship when facing the bow (forwards).

Port taxes Charges levied by the authorities at some ports of call, usually payable by the individual passenger, sometimes included in the final price of the cruise.

Repositioning cruises When cruise ships travel from one major cruising area to another with stops along the way at various ports. (For example, a ship travelling from the Caribbean at the end of the winter season to Alaska or Europe for the summer season.)

Round-trip cruises Also called **loop cruises**: the ship departs from and returns to the same port, which is referred to as the **home port** or **base port**. If the round-trip cruise is from a British port, it's referred to as an **ex-UK cruise**.

Ratings The rating given a ship is determined by the its level of accommodations, facilities, maintenance and service provided to its passengers. Ships that offer the ultimate in comfort and personalised service are called **luxury** ships (5★ in our book) and the atmosphere is usually described as 'formal' with passengers dressing up for dinner most evenings. These are also the most expensive ships to cruise on, although the price can vary considerably depending on the grade of cabin booked.

Next in rank are the **upper-mainstream** (4★+) ships. Their atmosphere is often 'semi-formal' with men wearing a jacket and tie to dinner most nights. Some upper-mainstream ships, usually those that appeal to a younger clientele, are classified as 'casual', with a fairly relaxed dress code in the dining room at dinnertime and a stronger emphasis on shipboard activities versus elegant service. Just below upper-mainstream in rank are **mainstream** (4★)ships, which offer slightly less attentive service.

Ships in the **budget** category (3★)are often older vessels which, although comfortable, lack the sparkle of the newer cruise ships or of the classic liners that are regularly refurbished to maintain their aura of luxury.

Some ships, such as expedition cruisers, sailing ships and river cruise vessels, are more difficult to rate because they fall into specialised categories which disallow a fair comparison between them and the larger ships.

Sister ships Ships that are identical in basic design and construction but usually with variations in internal layout, decor and public room features.

Space/passenger ratio A measure of how roomy or crowded a ship is. The ship's tonnage (total space capacity) divided by the total number of passengers equals the space/passenger ratio. 40+ is the ultimate in spaciousness; under 20 is high density.

Starboard On the right side of the ship when facing the bow (forwards).

Stateroom This is simply another term for **Cabin**.

Steward A waiter or cabin attendant on board.

Tonnage The overall size and capacity of the ship. A ship that measures more than 30,000 tons is a 'large' ship, 20,000 to 30,000 tons is a 'medium' ship and one less than 20,000 tons is 'small'. Ships that measure 70,000+ tons are called 'megaships'.

Index

143

K
KD River Cruises 94
Key West 60

L
land tours 41–42
laundry 13
Legend of the Seas 124
length of cruise 32–34, 45,
131–132
lifeboat drill 118–119

M
Madeira 27, 55
Main (River) 80
Malaysia 64
Martinique 61
meals 12, 48–49, 117–118
Mediterranean 18, 21,
24–25, 66–73; map 69
megaships 36
Mexico 30, 73
Mississippi 32, 128
Morocco 55–56
Moselle 80

N
New England 29
new ships 123–125
New Zealand 29, 65
newcomer cruises 39
Nile 16, 32, 67, 108–109;
see also Thomas Cook
Holidays
North American eastern
seaboard 29
Norway 75–78
Norwegian Coastal Voyage
94
Norwegian Cruise Lines
94–95

O
Oriana 30, 97–98, 125
Orient Lines 95–96
overland tours 18–19

P
P & O Cruises 96–100
Panama Canal 30, 74
passports and visas 110
peace and quiet 46–47
phone calls 111, 121
photography 16, 121–122
Portugal 71
Princess Cruises 100–103

Q
QE2 28, 87–88

R
ratings of ships and cruise
lines 82, 142
reading material 114–115
relaxation 7–8
reliability 11–12
Rhine 31, 79–80
Rhône 81
river cruises 17, 31–32, 37,
79–81, 91, 107
romance 9
Royal Caribbean Cruise
Line 103–105
Russia 78

S
sailing vessels 37
St Lucia 62
St Thomas 62
Samoa 65
San Juan 58
Scandinavia 18, 26–27,
75–78; map 76–77
Sea Goddess I and II
89–90
Seabourn Cruise Line
105–106
seasickness 50–51,
112–113
security 10–11
Seine 81
ships, types of 34–37,
123–125
shopping 13

shore activities and excursions 17, 19–21,
120–121
Silversea Cruises 106
Singapore 64
social activities 46–47
South Pacific 29–30,
65–66
Spain 71–72
special interest cruises
15–16, 40–41
special occasions 51; see
also honeymoons
Spice Island Cruises 108
staff 49–50, 118
star ratings 82, 142
Swan Hellenic 107–108
Sweden 78

T
tall ships see sailing vessels
Tampa 58
Thailand 64
theme cruises see special
interest cruises
Thomas Cook 129–130
Thomas Cook Holidays
108–109
Thomson Cruises 109
tipping 119–120
Tobago 62
tonnage 142
transatlantic cruises 28
travel agents 129–130,
137
travel documents
110–111
Tunisia 72
Turkey 72–73

V
vaccinations 112
Victoria 99–100

W
wildlife 21, 25